Adventures in Paradise

Exploring the Upper Connecticut Valley
of Vermont and New Hampshire
(On a Bicycle!)

Dick Mackay

FACULTY RIDGE BOOKS

For Paul Gerber, M.D.,
who would have liked it.

Library of Congress Cataloguing-in-Publication Data
Mackay, Dick
Adventures in Paradise, Exploring the Upper Connecticut Valley of Vermont & New Hampshire (On a Bicycle!)
Library of Congress Control Number: 2003094794
ISBN 0-9727768-0-X

Every effort has been made to provide up-to-date descriptions of possible hazards that may be encountered while using this book. Users are reminded that they alone are responsible for their own safety when on the road or trail, and that they bike, hike, or walk the routes described and shown in this book at their own risk. The authors, publishers, producers and editors of Adventures in Paradise assume no responsibility for any injury, misadventure, or loss occurring from use of the information contained herein. Read *Safety First* advisory on page 11.

Photographs: Dick Mackay
Front cover photo: North Thetford Rd., Lyme, N.H.
Back cover photo: Quechee; East Barnard, Vt.

Book Design, Tour Map Creation, Production: Final Proof Design & Publishing • Plainfield, N.H.
Editing: Getting Ink Done
Topographic maps: USGS
Photo scanning: K&L Color Graphics • White River Jct., Vt.

Faculty Ridge Books
Box 567
Hanover NH 03755
www.newbiking.com
Send comments and corrections to mail@newbiking.com

"Oh, the places you'll go!"
Dr. Seuss

Foreword

This book is the result of two gifts, each of which enthralled me from the moment I received it. The first was *Abandoned New England* by William F. Robinson, a book of photographs and essays. My brand new sister-in-law presented it to me for Christmas at the time of its publication nearly thirty years ago, and the world outside has never seemed the same since. The subtitle tells it all: *Its Hidden Ruins and Where to Find Them*. Fifteen years later, a Dartmouth student friend left her new bicycle in our garage over the summer. I'd always wanted to be a bike rider, but those "ten speeds" of the '70s were rolling advertisements for groin injury. Here was something different though—a mountain bike she called it. I thought it rode like a two-wheeled sports car. What torque! It got off the line like the Austin Healey of my youth. After effervescing over the pistachio lines of this knobby-tired thing for about a month, my wife gave me a silver Diamondback for our anniversary and I was immediately doing wheelies in the driveway. With topo maps from *College Supply* in Hanover in hand, off I pedaled to the dirt roads of Norwich, Thetford, and points north, east, west, and south. And the beauty of what I found brought tears to my eyes.

Now, as a bike rider, it's Christmas every day. This time, though, it's my turn to do the giving with this guide to the remarkable countryside of the Upper Valley region. Along with it comes a small dose of metaphysics, an idea that I call "New Biking."

Dutchmens Point? A recently discovered map suggests that Dutch explorers traveling up the Connecticut may have reached the mouth of the White River, left, as early as 1615.

The Talking Book

Paradise—the Upper Valley—is hardly unappreciated for its beauty, hardly unvisited by travelers, and hardly unknown to the outsider. But—and this is a BIG but—it is vastly under-explored and under-recognized by its very own people. This is what we are going to change. First of all, though, where exactly is the Upper Valley? Opinions differ, but throwing an anchor overboard where the White and Connecticut Rivers meet is a good place to start. The stern of your kayak or canoe will soon slue around downstream and you'll be facing north by northwest. Now, hold your right arm out at a forty-five degree angle and bend your left as far back as it will go. That's the Upper Valley, including the southern half of Hartland, over your left shoulder, and Plainfield and the northern half of Cornish, which are behind your head.

All in all, the region takes in the drainage of the Connecticut, upriver forty miles to the Ammonoosuc and Wells Rivers systems in the towns of Newbury and Haverhill, plus the White, Ottauquechee, and Mascoma Rivers systems to the northwest, west, and east. All told, the geography of the Connecticut and its tributaries—rather than Vermont's reputation for bicycling (and enlightenment)—account for the fact that twenty-eight of the tours in this book are on the west side of the river and only eight on the east. What about the other four? They share the best of both worlds.

OVERTAKING THE PAST

The premise of this book is in the title; the region happens to be an ideal place to ride a bike. But forget that for a moment. Think of this twenty-by-forty-mile ensemble of rivers and hillsides as a Great Book of history and natural science, a Big Print Book that is always open, and a Talking Book that is always speaking. If New England is America's attic, then the Upper Valley is an old family album high up on a cobwebbed shelf. Oh, we know our past is there between the covers all right, but we have forgotten the faces and places inside it and how they relate to us.

The main reason we've seen so little of our nearby world is that most of us live on paved roads down in the valleys and we stick to them. Even if we do live up on Podunk Road in Hartford, we have no occasion to explore Podunk up beyond Old City in Strafford. Oh sure, both are deep in the boondocks, but how about the posh Loop in even more posh South Woodstock? Ever stumble upon it and wonder where its fancy pants came from? Or *East* Lebanon—ever hear of it? Probably not, but for half a century East Lebanon was far more prominent than the city we know today. And these days you can ride a bicycle to its forgotten site on a flat, dedicated pathway and explore its artifacts entirely on your own. Greek Revival architecture and a stone pyramid in West Fairlee—why? And why does the map bother to identify a West Fairlee *Center*? There are no people there at all. Where did they go? In North Haverhill, what is unmistakably a depot from the steam locomotive era sits in a village neighborhood. But where's the railroad?

Many of us remember that first time we went birding or looked at the stars through a telescope. How can all those fantastically colored warblers be out there without our knowing it?! They must have always been there, flying all around, veritable air fleets of them in May—but I did not see! Stars, billions of stars—look at them up there! Is there life elsewhere in the universe? How could there *not* be? This is the kind of unnoticed world of the past that is hiding in plain sight—right outside, right here, right now—in the Upper Valley. And we are going to go find it on a bicycle.

Afoot and light-hearted I take to the open road,
Healthy, free, the world before me,
The long brown path before me,
Leading wherever I choose.
  Walt Whitman, *Song of the Open Road*

THE WHYS AND WHEREFORES OF PARADISE

Besides New Biking, the exercise of body and mind this book celebrates is founded on two notions. The first is as old as the hills themselves: *geography is destiny*. Here in the New England uplands, we have not dozens, but hundreds of back roads, discontinued roads, Jeep roads, horse roads, and impassable abandoned tracks that practically nobody but the few residents who live on them (and the UPS driver) ever see. Why are they there?

When white men settled this region beginning in the 1760s, their goal was not the wet, often-impenetrable valleys, but the drier uplands where the first frost came later. (What about the priceless riverside bottomlands known as intervales? Gone to a few insider favorites of the colonial governors.) Had those settlers not gone uphill, more than half the roads we will tour would never have been gouged out of wilderness. Look at it this way: when you're gazing up and down thirty miles of the

Connecticut River Valley from the crown of Pattrell Road in Norwich, the question is not only what New Hampshire peaks you're marveling at, but why there's a road up here at all. To our enduring fascination, Pattrell Road—like Joe Ranger Road in Pomfret, Silloway Road in East Randolph, and a hundred others—goes *from* nowhere *to* nowhere. Living in New England, we know the geography of stonewalls pretty well, but it's those bends in the roads to everywhere and nowhere that ask to be followed and gotten to the top and bottom of.

Then there are the abandoned mines and mills, the cellar holes and old cemeteries, and the apple trees struggling in old pastures gone to juniper and junk pine. We know that ours is a landscape that can only mime. But mute as it may be, we can still listen to what it has to say, provided we are willing to get close to it.

That brings us to the second idea about our "built" environment—a pastoral landscape that thrived a century or more ago and then became largely obsolete. *Wealth builds, poverty preserves.* Like the surplus roads, the truly lovely time-capsule towns and villages that nestle everywhere here—Lyme Center, Newbury, Strafford, and Pomfret, to name only a few—simply demand an explanation. Some flowering of wealth built them, but what queer orientation of the planets put them on ice for a century or more? We know why we are here (mostly because this is a better place to be than where we were before), but how did the happy accident that is the handmade antique countryside around us come to pass? Paradise, what are your whys and wherefores? That's what we're going to find out. We are going to overtake this past of ours and we're going to do it on a bicycle. Convinced yet?

The past is never dead. It's not even past.
    William Faulkner

New Biking
THE FRIENDLIEST MACHINE, A BICYCLE BUILT FOR ALL, 1885-1905

Craze with a capital C is the only way to describe the new bicycling of a century ago. Previously, as the enthusiast sport known as "wheeling," bicycle riding meant collarbone-breaking skydives off expensive high-wheel machines built exclusively for men, most of whom were blue bloods. This all changed in 1886 with the development in Coventry, England, of the Rover "safety" bike, the common two-wheeler—an event similar in impact on late Victorian society to the debut of the personal computer a century later. The Rover safety, with its in-line wheels of equal size, chain drive, and direct steer from handlebars to front fork, ignited the first great fad in American history, just ahead of the postcard. During the Gay Nineties, one-third of U.S. Patent Office applications were bicycle related. And as soon as the cost of a machine dropped below $100, safety bikes became available to the masses.

To be associated with bicycling in this period—as with the debut of the Internet a century later—was to be considered cutting edge. The machine itself, like the PC, became identified with the economic and social future of America. In 1897 New York mayoral candidates fell over one another trying to line up the bicycle vote, with Tammany Hall putting out a daily newspaper that promoted both cycling and the party's standard bearer. America's first superstar athletes were men who raced each other around wooden tracks and cinder-covered ovals, sometimes for twenty hours a day, vying for large cash prizes and the right to endorse roll-your-own

My New Bike, c. 1900
Location unknown

tobacco and alcohol-laced patent medicines. The advertising, promotion, and news coverage of bicycle competitions fully equaled today's motor-racing hullabaloo.

But no one profited from bicycle-mania more than America's largest underclass—women. Although for a short time men tried to retain control by endorsing the tandem, a massive yearning for independence in the outdoors set women astride their own two wheelers. Bloomers, the softwear of the international "rational dress for women" campaign, were all the rage, with "bicycle corsets" the antecedent of the sports bra. Bluenoses were horrified at how cycling empowered women, until the president of the Womens Christian Temperance Union published a memoir of life on the road with the underwhelming title *How I Learned to Ride a Bicycle*. As the first outside activity pursued by women independent of their husbands, the bicycle craze prefigured the drive for the vote and women's rights.

At the height of the craze in 1897, two million bicycles were sold. But in a remarkable parallel to the present day, discounting by department stores—the Wal-Marts of the day—began to cut into profits and make bicycles a mere commodity. Profits of leading manufacturers began to go flatter than one of the new Dunlop pneumatic tyres that had picked up a horseshoe nail. Bicycle frame producers, accessory makers, and rubber companies formed a cartel to fight off the discounters, but it was too late. Worse, the first powered two-wheeler, the "motor-cycle," was introduced the very next year. Shortly afterward, the wild success of the friendliest mechanical invention of all time was taken to a third level by, among others, a young Michigan bicycle mechanic named Henry Ford.

NEW BIKING, 1985 TO FOREVER

The fad didn't last. In America, by the time of WWI, the horseless carriage had relegated bicycling to children, a very few diehard enthusiasts, and those who couldn't afford a $500 Model T flivver. It would be sixty years of balloon-tired Hopalong Cassidy cruisers, funky Lemon Peelers and Orange Krates, and leaden Raleighs before the heavens aligned themselves in favor of meaningful bicycling once again. Then, out West, tinkerers developed a machine to climb the dusty tracks up Mt. Talmapais in Marin County on the Bay: the

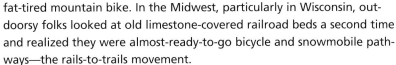

Point of View

Let me tell you what I think of bicycling. It has done more to emancipate women than anything else in the world. It gives a woman a feeling of freedom and self-reliance. I stand and rejoice every time I see a woman ride by on a wheel. She is the picture of free, untrammeled womanhood.

Susan B. Anthony

fat-tired mountain bike. In the Midwest, particularly in Wisconsin, out-doorsy folks looked at old limestone-covered railroad beds a second time and realized they were almost-ready-to-go bicycle and snowmobile path-ways—the rails-to-trails movement.

Combine this new equipment with these new venues, add federal trans-portation "enhancement" funding beginning in '92, and the result, within just a few years, is the sales of millions of mountain bicycles and reinvention of the sport as a mass upscale activity. Fanny-enhancing spandex was already out there, which probably helped too. Boosting the New Biking movement from its unheralded rebirth were—and are—nonprofit orgs like the D.C.-based Rails to Trails Conservancy; the East Coast Greenway, promot-ing a Calais, Maine to Key West path; and Adventure Cycling, which was created to promote cross-country touring at the time of the Bicentennial. (World leader: Velo Quebec. See velo.qc.ca) Since the mid '80s, hundreds of local bootstrap organizations across the country have joined the effort, helping to create thousands of miles of dedicated community bikeways and on-road signed routes to meet the demand of New Bicyclists.

By the late '90s, another tech twist broadened and reinforced bicycling's appeal: the hybrid machine. With upright handlebars, mid-width tires, water bottle cage, rear rack for a lunch, and front bag for sunscreen and car keys, the hybrid emerged as the everywhere, everywoman piece of

"I made it!"
New bikers, Rt. 12-A, Plainfield;
Mt. Ascutney in the background.

hardware. The indoor health club workout known as Spinning should get some credit too for keeping us northerners focused on summer while staying saddle-ready over the winter. New Biking became a continuum, from training wheels on flat rail-trails, to road biking for logo-plastered, aging baby boomers needing an (imagined) low-impact serotonin fix to replace all that jogging they used to "enjoy."

But there was more to the sport's popularity than just sweat, particularly for women. For those who hopped over the cross-bar and became New Bikers, what was beside the road was just as important as what was under the wheels; the brain, as well as the butt, had to be put in gear. Now, with appropriate hardware between our legs and a yen for the lore of the countryside between our ears, *Adventures in Paradise* presents the software for New Biking. Here is a menu for your savoring—a banquet of backcountry and river-bottom roads in the three-star Upper Valley, surely one of New Biking's New Jerusalems. But it's not quite all bread and circuses in this Paradise. Along with the lengthy bill of fare comes a special new tool essential for the *pitched* battle ahead: the philosophy of the *walking* hill.

WALKING HILLS

When you, as a New Biker, come to a hill that is too steep to climb, you will dismount, unclasp your helmet, and take a breath. Then you will mount the hill on foot, taking your own sweet time doing so. And what a stroke of luck! You will now be adventuring in one of the many outdoor rooms of Paradise and you will be doing so at less than one mile per hour. (I win!)

Immersion in this heavenly countryside begins the moment you get off your bike. The first thing you'll notice is a gurgling down in the swale along the road. That's the brook you and the road have been following for a ways—the road having done so without your help for two hundred or more years. The next sound most likely will be that of an insistent bird. If there are open lands and fence posts nearby, it will be the sputtery bickering of a kingbird patrolling his territory. The loud and demanding wheep! from the tip of a high branch is the call of a cousin, the great crested flycatcher.

If you stop on the walking hill to wait for a companion or take in the view, more amiable members of the tyrant flycatcher family will soon flit silently onto a wire. Bobbing there for a moment, the phoebe and mate will eventually announce themselves with contented *fee-bree* notes. Their teacup-sized, moss-lined nest is hidden on the graying joist of an old barn or an unrecognized-for-what-it-was milk house nearby. Overhead, above the trees and farm buildings, battlements of pillowy cumulus will rise silently in the west.

By the time you're standing in the shade a little farther up the hill, a car may come by. You will wonder if the people inside think you're odd or perhaps lost and out of your element on such an incline. But don't worry, these feelings will only last a few years. By that time, pushing a bicycle uphill on the back roads of the Upper Valley will have joined another outdoor activity once thought rather silly—jogging—as mainstream. Walking hills—the best thing to happen to bicycling since the derailleur. Hey, everybody's doing it. Walk on!

A Walking Hill, Indian Pond Rd., Orford. Great fun, even in November.

Do not, as some ungracious pastors do, show me the steep and thorny way to heaven.
    Hamlet, I, iii, 47

Finding Your Way

Who has not spread out a map on the table and felt its promise of places to go and things to see and do?
John Noble Wilford, *The Mapmakers*, 1981

TOPO MAPS

The tours in this book are laid out on standard-issue U.S. Geological Survey topographical instruments— topo maps—of a style that is almost a century old. (You say *TOP-oh*, I say *TOE-poh*.) Each 20"x 26" paper map covers a rectangular chunk of the American countryside six and a half miles wide by a little over nine miles high. Laid side by side, about thirty-three thousand of these quadrangles, or "quads," cover the lower forty-eight states, which explains why updated versions of them are issued so infrequently. The North Hartland quad, for instance, is dated 1959, with "photorevision" in 1980. Newbury dates from 1973, and South Royalton 1981, with "photoinspection" two years after that. Yes, the interstates have all been added, first in red, then in magenta for a time, and now in red once again.

But with so little revision, the softly pastelled topos can be appreciated as charmingly dated survivors of the artfulness of an earlier era, while not being so antique as to be obsolete. As design critic Philip Nobel recently observed, ever since all Terra Incognitas disappeared from the globe, "cartography has been practiced in ever colder realms of objectivity." Warmth and a bit of intrigue survive in the spring-green USGS sheets, along with the signposts of the past we are about to seek out— the enigmatic Copper Flat, Devils Den, Hell Hollow, and Fish Market.

Cue the Ride . . . Tri-Town Loop

The Tri-Town map opposite includes most of the symbols and route markings used in Tours 1-40. Sections of the Loop are in various stages of development, with the desirable Lebanon-West Lebanon connection likely to be finished by 2006—depending on public involvement, of course. Shoulder widths vary.

Biking and walking trails in and around the feature known as the Lebanon Dome developed informally in the 1980s from a network of power line corridors and access roads. The trail map is taken from a sketch prepared by volunteers. Parking is available at most access points.

1. Mt. Support Road, preferred DHMC-Lebanon bike route. Access to Lebanon Dome bike trails off DHMC access roads, School for Lifelong Learning, Old Pine Tree Cemetery Rd., Wilder Dam, and Sachem Village.

2. Northern Railtrail, downtown Lebanon – APD Hospital area.

3. Proposed railtrail and rail-with-trail extension to Glen Rd., West Lebanon.

4. Rotary skateboard park. Path to South Main St./NH Rt.12-A, sidewalks to West Lebanon proper.

5. Proposed riverside greenway, cross-river link via shared-use railroad bridge.

6. US Rt.5, White River Jct. to Wilder.

7. Wilder bikeway. Proposed shoulder improvements to Norwich town line.

8. Montshire Museum of Science, Conte Wildlife Refuge HQ, trails, river access. See Tour 1 for suggested route into Hanover.

MAP KEY

16 Tour Number

Trail/Route

Alternate Routes

Walking/Hiking Path

✕✕✕ Dangerous Riding

3 Directional Aid Points of Interest

A Historical Interest

View

360° View

AT Appalachian Trail

c.s. Convenience Store

HOL Height of Land

Easy Ride

Moderate Ride

Difficult Ride

Hill

Big Hill

Walking Hill

1 Tour Location Marker

Scale: Varies due to reduction; most maps 2" = 1m.

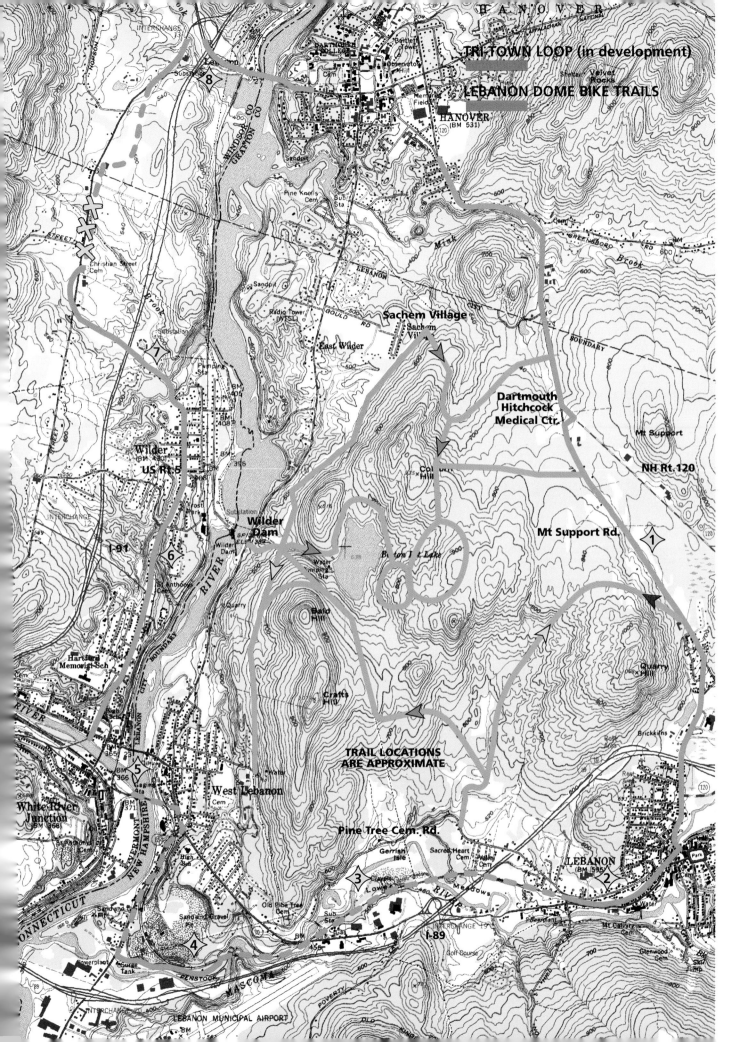

TRI-TOWN LOOP (in development)

Shelter   Velvet
Rocks

LEBANON DOME BIKE TRAILS

HANOVER
(BM 531)

Sachem Village

Dartmouth
Hitchcock
Medical Ctr.

Mt Support

NH Rt. 120

Mt Support Rd.

⬥ 1

Wilder
Dam

Wilder
US Rt. 5

Burton Test Lake

I-91

⬥ 6

Bald
Hill

⬥ 7

⬥ 8

Hartford
Memorial Sch

Crafts
Hill

Quarry
Hill

Brickkilns

TRAIL LOCATIONS
ARE APPROXIMATE

⬥ 5

West Lebanon

LEBANON
(BM 595)

⬥ 2

White River
Junction
(BM 368)

Pine Tree Cem. Rd.

Gerrish
Isle

Sacred Heart
Cem

⬥ 3

⬥ 4

I-89

LEBANON MUNICIPAL AIRPORT

But what is most important about topos in a practical context is that the data (now available on CD) is in the public domain. That is not to say the mapmaking was easy; each sheet is a separate mega-file, and the merging together of maps for tours that span two, three, or four quads is a byte-crunching task for anyone's desktop hard drive. Cartography fans should also be aware of the metric/U.S. customary measurement pickle that arose during the '80s among the maps in any one region, including the N.H./Vt. area. In its bureaucratic wisdom, the USGS began to combine two side-by-side quads and reissue them in hastily drawn metric 1:25000 scale, rather than the 1:24000 format that had been used for decades. Within a few years, Americans told their government in no uncertain terms that metric was for foreigners, and the King's foot was hurriedly reinstated. The metric double-quads are still out there, however, leaving the hiker and hunter out in the woods where maps of different scales meet up the creek.

Lastly, in most cases the topo maps in the book have been shrunk by almost a third to fit. Even at that reduction, this book is probably the largest bike guide ever published. The Norwich suite of tours, 17–19 and Tour 35, Royalton, wouldn't fit and are turned 90 degrees. For an example of a topo reproduced at 100 percent, see Tour 12, East of Eden. Scale-wise, on most maps consider two inches to equal about a mile.

MAPS TO TAKE ALONG ON THE BIKE

Besides bringing photocopies of the tour you plan to take, the *state-issued* N.H. and Vermont highway maps will be helpful out in the field. That's not because they're free, but because they are easier to follow and more pleasant to look at than commercial maps. Get two. Keep one for the car, and cut out the sections covering the Upper Valley from the other map for on-board use. To be fully equipped, outfit yourself with N.H. and Vermont editions of the invaluable DeLorme *Atlas & Gazetteer* series. At four times the scale of the USGS topographical maps used here, the proprietary DeLorme topos cover a much larger area per page. Note that a few—but only a few—road names in DeLorme have become obsolete since the Universal 911-prompted revisions, particularly where a road crosses town lines.

Snowmobile maps, which put the backcountry rambler on signed trails that see little or no recreational use after the snow melts, also can be a valuable resource. Find them at *vast.org* and *nhsa.com*, keeping in mind that most of these trails traverse private property. Note also that snowmobile trails are usually better suited to woods tramping and vigorous walking than biking. (Snowmobile maps sold in plastic bags at CStores are nearly worthless, by the way.)

Finally, the pocket-sized topographical maps and guides to various popular outdoor venues in N.H. and Vermont created by *mapadventures.com* are some of the best of the genre. If you can find one, the handsome but out-of-print Randolph area sheet prepared for the (defunct?) White River Valley Trails organization in the '90s is unexcelled for ease-of-use, accuracy, and depth. It covers a marvelous selection of inspiring routes that beckon from beyond this book's latitude.

GETTING LOST

Imagine what it was like for the first cyclists trying to string a route between towns along the rude dirt roads of the 1890s. Road maps as we know them didn't exist. It wasn't until "filling stations" and promotional oil company maps debuted that the navigational needs of country travelers were attended to. Worse, roads weren't even numbered until the states took over the through routes, beginning around 1915. The railroads of the day certainly had no interest in acquainting wheelmen with a road system other than their own. When local people traveled, they often did so by rail, leaving them with limited knowledge of roads beyond their own neighborhoods.

But at least the railroad lines went somewhere. In the formative years of wheeling, the roads of steel, along with telegraph and telephone poles, proved to be the best directional indicator for the next outpost of civilization. Betwixt and between, lonely pedalers could also rely on country folk to know where—and what—the next town was. And since farm people were usually out and about, one could also hope to be set right over the fence at the next farmhouse, just around the next bend.

Today the situation is much improved, but let's be realistic: human nature hasn't changed in the intervening hundred years. Women can't read maps and men don't listen to directions, so between them, sooner or later, everybody's lost. Now, this is not such a bad thing when you're behind the wheel of a car; you just reverse course in the next driveway. (The one with the "No Turning" sign, which tells you you're not so dumb after all. So many people get lost around there that they have to post a sign.) On a bike, though, it's different; every cyclist's worst nightmare is riding three miles out of the way *downhill*.

Still, getting lost is more of a challenge than it used to be. Although missing a turn remains common, thanks to local road renaming associated with the Universal 911 program of the early '90s, getting your bearings out in the field has never been easier. While much has been lost artistically with the removal of the old directionals, what we got in return is new, accurate signage that reassures the wandering traveler at the most obscure side-road in the wilderness. That said, human nature hasn't changed since U911 was adopted, so, in general, we're just about back to where we were before. Same problem, all right, with the same solution. Head out in mixed company, allowing the gentlemen to use the map to plan the route. When you get lost, have the ladies wave down the next passerby for directions.

And you may ask yourself What is that beautiful house?
And you may ask yourself Where does that highway go?
And you may ask yourself Am I right? . . . Am I wrong?
And you may tell yourself MY GOD! . . . WHAT HAVE I DONE?
        Talking Heads, *Once in a Lifetime*

LAY OF THE LAND

As noted, geography is destiny. More than thirty of the forty tours in this book begin in the south and head north, upstream along the watercourses, following the always evident trail of the retreating glacier. So powerful is the organizing role of upstream geography that conceptually one could say life in the Connecticut River Valley of Vermont and New Hampshire is determined by it. In the morning, life trickles down and south to the valley floor where the flat land lies; in the evening, it migrates north and back up the hills where it roosts for the night. We ride in reverse, beginning our quests down low along the river valleys, then strike out for the heights in sweaty search of our forebearers, the ones that struggled up to the hill farms and stayed there.

Applied science figures in the south-to-north routing, as well. It keeps the summer sun off our face and puts the prevailing south-southwest wind at our back, no small blessing in July.

Where to start? Visitors to the area are likely to be attracted first to the two premiere Upper Valley outdoor rooms, Hanover and Woodstock, as well they might. Hanover and its suburb of Norwich are the jumping off place for touring the Connecticut, with Woodstock and its companion towns of Quechee and Pomfret at the heart of the inland Vermont empire. But Fairlee and Bradford on the Conn., South Royalton on the White, Hartland on the Ottauquechee and Lebanon on the Mascoma are not to be overlooked. All have seven-day-a-week pre-flight services, casual parking and in-town green space of their own, except Bradford, which has a high falls instead. As a measure of how civilized the region is overall, cyclists will never find themselves more than five miles from a good bakery or ten miles from a real boiled bagel.

We ourselves sometimes forget that the road serves other needs. For untold thousands of years we traveled on foot over rough paths and dangerously unpredictable roads, not simply as peddlers or commuters or tourists, but as men and women for whom the path and road stood for some intense experience: freedom, new human relationships, a new awareness of the landscape. The road offered a journey into the unknown that could end up allowing us to discover who we were and where we belonged.
        John Brinkerhoff Jackson, Founder of *Landscape* magazine, 1992

ROAD TERMINOLOGY

Town road means town maintained, with either a dirt or paved surface. Historically, town roads have been categorized by class, but field observations over recent decades indicate these classes don't mean much nowadays. Either a road is kept up to a certain passable level, whatever that might be locally, or it isn't. Only the *Class VI* designation "not maintained, or abandoned" continues to be descriptive. But that doesn't mean a lot either in terms of bike- or walk-ability. One might think the 1930s were the heyday of abandonment, but not so. Locally, towns were "throwing up" roads as late at the 1970s, when the last of the Depression Era hill people moved downhill to the cemeteries. Yes, some Class VI roads are ready to be logged, but others are entirely Mini ready. As with the safety advisory below, the terminology used here is meant to inform as *Fully-equipped for the countryside.*
Brownsville Rd., Hartland.

to some of the wide array of conditions to be found on these so-called town highways. Note also these conditions may vary from what the topos seem to indicate visually. That is to be expected, given the age of the maps.

The joyous path called the *woods road* is often grassy and lacks extensive washouts. A *Jeep road* is passable, but probably only during drier periods. Ultimately, erosion will finish off a Jeep road and then it becomes whatever you wish to call it; a *horse road* perhaps. For our purposes, *trails* are roads that have grown up with foliage; many of them are the remnants of old farm roads. Lowland sections of the Appalachian Trail often follow what were once tracks to the back forty—the path of least resistance in the 1930s for originator Benton MacKaye and his followers. (No bikes on the AT, please.)

Note that impassable Class VI roads don't always stay that way. After fifty years or so, a stumpage buyer will cruise through the second growth alongside, a skidder to follow. Collapsed culverts will be replaced, a few loads of gravel dumped in the worst of the bathtubs, and a bit of grading done. After the log trucks have emptied the woods, the town may even assume maintenance once again. Back country riders who come upon these logging operations the second time around can be in for quite a shock at this omen of subdivision.

DEGREE OF DIFFICULTY

Easy, moderate, demanding, difficult—what do they mean? More like the compounding Richter scale than a standard gradation, new riders will find routes rated moderate to be an altogether different experience than those rated easy. They are much harder—period. In all cases, tours should be evaluated beforehand from the more detailed notes accompanying each.

Easy means flat, like the rail trails or routes with well-spaced, manageable hills.

Moderate rides may have a formidable walking hill or two, but riders who have a season of outings under their glutes will be able to find great pleasure in them.

Demanding routes feature many hills, and only those who cycle regularly will enjoy them. This can also mean rough, wet, or changeable conditions, or that the road is abandoned or not town-maintained year-round. See the "Safety Advisory" for a broader description of field conditions you may encounter.

Difficult. Not necessarily for gearheads in terms of mileage, a difficult ride encounters many big hills, plus some or all of the road conditions noted above. How hilly is it around here? Well, of all the tours that Montana-based Adventure Cycling operates, its Tour Vermont outing is rated the most difficult. (Connecticut Valley—what valley?)

I lift up mine eyes to the hills. From whence does my help come?
    Psalms, 22A

ESTIMATING TIME

On a flat, paved road, the average new rider can expect to cover about twelve miles an hour. But there are no flats around here, except for the railtrails, and they are not paved. For general purposes, estimate a twenty-mile paved ride, like Tour 1 (Hanover to East Thetford and return), will take about two hours. Unless you consider yourself a "biker," however, you can almost double the 20m./2 hr. estimate for tours that involve two or more walking hills, particularly if the day means to be hot. At four or more hours per ride, outings can then be estimated in terms of "being out for the afternoon," a wonderful prospect in its own right.

EQUIPMENT

Bike shops know bikes, and how to fit them. There are four professionally staffed operations in the Upper Valley; one in Hanover and Lebanon, and two in Woodstock. Let them put you on an appropriately

East Topsham

sized machine, that's their forte. Hybrids, sometimes known as "comfort bikes", make good sense for anyone launching a New Biking career here in Paradise. Buying a helmet goes without saying, but too many new bikers forget to protect their eyes. Even though June bugs only come out after dark, use eyewear on every ride; bumblebees are diurnal, after all. Gloves? Why not, they soak up sweat. Finally, what about those cycling shirts, are they really necessary? No, not right away. Same with pedal clips and fancy shoes. Start out with toe baskets; go to roadie equipment later. As for the claims of various food supplement and additive manufacturers, these products have no anti-gravity effect whatsoever.

SAFETY FIRST

Safety considerations are at the forefront of any sane bicycle rider's planning. Wear a helmet, tend to your brakes, ride right, see and be seen—these fundamentals carry across the spectrum of bicycling venues and surfaces, as they always have and always will. To these basics must be added this: when it comes to the road—any and all roads—plan on anything and every-

thing. You must be mindful, for instance, that while an abandoned road displays obvious hazards, the reassuring ten-foot wide paved shoulders of an "improved" highway like NH Rt.10 are no less accident-prone. Slippery rocks, branches and hidden obstructions await the fat tire on the former; while acorns, cracked asphalt and broken glass lurk ahead of the skinny tire on the latter.

Given the combination of hard and softer surfaces on many of the tours, a conspicuous concern must be the transition from paved to dirt and vice versa. Hazards at these spots include asphalt made slick by loose sand, puddles that hide potholes and stones, jagged lips, broken-off chunks of pavement, loose tire-grabbing mud . . . ad infinitum. Also expect to encounter washboard at these transitions (and at dips in many, many dirt roads), a condition that creates vibration that will rip the grips right out of your hands at any speed faster than a skunk's trot.

Again, though, there can be no complete list of hazards, either here in the Upper Valley or anywhere else. Windy days may drop branches to the shoulder, the town road agent may turn up cobbles or create soft shoulders with his grader, a witless young dog may run out under your front wheel—imagine any of these turning up as you soar downhill on that first really warm spring day. Whammo! and you're over the handlebars and in rehab. Bottom line: *pay attention!*

Along these lines, one new roadside phenomenon requires mention: shoulder peds. In recent years walking and jogging against traffic has become somewhat common, but who should yield when peds and cyclists meet head on is as yet unset-tled. For several reasons it would appear that foot traffic should

Safety First, US Rt.4, White River. Riding single file inside the white line. Good going, kids!

give way. It seems evident that those who can see oncoming traffic, who can adjust to uneven ground off the pavement and who are moving slower should yield. Agreed? OK, then consider it settled.

Aboard, at a ship's helm,
A young steerman, steering with care.
     Walt Whitman

Vigorous Walks

Thanks to a recent uptick in regional trail building, opportunities for walks, hikes, climbs and woods rambles will soon be numerous enough to be worthy of a guidebook of their own. (*Paradise Underfoot*, perhaps?) In the meantime, plenty of useful material exists, particularly in the way of thorough field guides to nearby mountains and the Appalachian Trail. But finding good maps to other less popular areas requires scurrying around. Begin with snowmobiling trail maps. After mud season these sheets become peerless pathfinders for back country explorers, with the proviso that warm weather access to what is usually private property is not often spelled out. As for simpler-to-follow on-road outings, several can be improvised from maps in this book, with a number of suggested best bets appearing below. If you are map-savvy, do-it-yourself route planning using individual store-bought topos on paper or CD is certainly possible, if not entirely practical, as many roads go unnamed. Consult Northern Cartographic's *Vermont Road Atlas* instead, which is superior to the DeLorme Gazetteer for this task. (No good equivalent exists for N.H.) Note that the road walks below were chosen because they permit the one defining feature of a good stroll—the ability for two or three people to proceed abreast. Hey, when you're walking that walk, you've got to be able to talk that talk.

TOWN WALKS

Woodstock. For over a century trails in Billings Park on Mt. Tom have distinguished Woodstock as a premiere regional venue for ardent pedestrians. Creation of the adjoining Marsh-Billings-Rockefeller National Historic Park in the 1990s vaulted the town into national prominence as both a Valhalla for strollers and an outdoor museum of Victorian attitudes about nature. Carriage roads, paths, trails, overlooks, picturesque outcrops, cool springs—the civilized slopes of Mt. Tom are unrivaled in their 19th century character. And now there's more, as antique paths up Mt. Peg— just south of town—have recently been added to the feast. The National Park Service cheerfully presents a superb map to all of this at the Billings Farm Visitors Center. Grab and *go*.

Hanover. A bronze plate at the Hanover Inn Corner marks the western entry of the Appalachian Trail into New Hampshire. Use this landmark as a recommended point of departure for the popular stroll through the campus to a loop of Occom Pond. Further explorations into the wilds of Pine Park and the Vale of Tempe can be enjoyed by following dog walkers from the head of the pond through the adjoining golf course. A slick, GPS-generated Hanover Trails sheet issued in 2003 (Town Office) will direct you to at least fifty more all-season outings throughout the town. In the tourist season, a useful Hanover/Norwich map can be manually downloaded from the conical kiosk on the Dartmouth Green. For only two bucks this map can't be beat, as it will orient one to about two-thirds of the region covered by this book.

DIRT ROAD WALKS

Norwich. Improvise loops from the map for Tours 16-19, or from the first-rate town ConCom trail map available at the Clerk's office in the village. Suggested walks: Bragg Hill Rd./Dutton Hill Rd. loop; or the less hilly Upper Turnpike/Needham Rd./Turnpike loop.

Pomfret. The old farm country to the west of Pomfret-up-the-Hill and Hewitts Corners is crosshatched by old dirt roads that beg to be investigated. Try this 5m. clockwise loop from the Town Hall: Webster Hill Rd./Hidden Ridge Rd./Hewitt Hill Rd./Johnson Rd. See Tour 31.

Barnard. A loop of similar length around Silver Lake leaves Barnard via North Road. Then TH54 (Class VI)/Royalton Tpke./Twin Farms/Stage Rd. See Tour 33.

Also note the **Lake Morey Loop**, a five-mile paved walk with associated short hikes. See Tour 3.

APPALACHIAN TRAIL WALKS

Car spotting at major road crossings permits easy section walking of the AT. Pick up a map at the Dartmouth Outing Club office, Robinson Hall on the Green.

West to east, approximate lengths of major segments are: Prosper Rd., Woodstock to County Rd., Pomfret, 2.5m. County Rd. to West Hartford bridge, 9m. West Hartford to Norwich, 7.5m. Dartmouth Green to Two Mile Rd./Etna, 7m. Two Mile Rd. over Moose Mt. (2100') to Goose Pond Rd., Lyme, 8m. Goose Pond Rd. to Dartmouth Skiway, Lyme Center, 5m.

Railtrail Walks

All railtrails walks are pleasant, these are some of the most scenic sections. Water is almost always nearby, so in May and June you will find the birding excellent and insect repellent worth its weight in gold. Distances are round trip. **Note:** The Northern Railtrail offers the best surface for **handicap accessible** outings. Cross Vermont Trail, Tour 9 - *Walk A*, is also wheelchair friendly, as are Oliverian/Blackmount, Tour 11 - *Walk A* and *Walk C*.

NORTHERN RAILTRAIL

TOUR 7 *Walk A.* Begin at the trailside parking lot on Riverside Drive in Lebanon, near the Packard Covered Bridge. Walk east a mile to twin railroad bridges, where Mill Road intersects. Loop back via Mill Road, an old section of the Concord Turnpike (think 1825 cattle drives to Boston), now closed to traffic, as it follows the opposite bank of the Mascoma River. Two miles plus.

Walk B. Park at Ice House Rd., Cue 4, off US Rt.4. Walk east along Mascoma Lake to scenic rock cutting at Cue 5, a fine picnic spot. Freight cars from a 1960s wreck are said to be still in the water below. Three miles.

Walk C. Walk east from Enfield Village center to Baltic Mill and dam. Note old depot, now the FAST squad HQ. Fire station opposite was built as a creamery. About a mile.

TOUR 8 *Walk A.* Park at West Canaan, Cue 1. Walk east to train wreck site, with interpretation. Head-on collision on the night of Sept. 15, 1907 killed 27, mostly Canadian families returning home from a fair. Two miles plus.

Walk B. Park at Tewksbury Pond, Grafton. Walk west to rock cut in Orange. Please don't pick the lilies. Two miles.

CROSS VERMONT TRAIL

TOUR 9 *Walk A.* Park at Ricker Pond, Cue 1. Walk west any distance. Kettle Pond and return is about 8 miles.

Walk B. Park at top of Depot Rd. in Marshfield, Cue 5. Walk east to views at Bailey Pond, one and a half miles.

TOUR 10 *Walk A.* Walk west from Blue Mountain High School to new-in-'03 I-91 bike/ped underpass and on to Boltonville. Three miles plus.

Walk B. Park at granite sheds in South Ryegate, Cue 3. Cross US Rt.302 to Brown Drive. Walk west any distance. Groton and return, about six miles.

Walk C. Blue Mountain Trail, off the rail corridor behind the High School. See Tour 10, Cue 1. Two miles.

OLIVERIAN/BLACKMOUNT BRANCH RAILTRAIL

TOUR 11 *Walk A.* E. Haverhill to Oliverian Pond, Cue 5 to 6. During black fly season none but the brave venture here. Five miles plus.

Walk B. Haverhill. Entry off Ladd St. or County Rd. (if gate open), half a mile north of Haverhill. Walk any distance. Unlikely ruins of massive stone viaduct border a cornfield two and a half miles north.

Walk C. Woodsville. Park where NH Rt.135 crosses railtrail, south of drive-in theater. Walk south to views of Howard Island from near County calaboose. Three and a half miles. See Woodsville map, Tour 5 Continuation.

TIMOTHY DWIGHT AND HIS TRAVELS

Timothy Dwight, patron saint of Connecticut Valley travelers, took it upon himself to make annual inspection tours of New England and neighboring regions from 1795 to 1815—America's formative years. According to Barbara Solomon, who edited his Travels in the 1960s, Dwight's purpose was to describe and explain the changing landscape he saw before him, as well as to correct erroneous impressions popularized in Europe by foreign visitors. Well suited for the task as president of Yale College, Dwight believed he was the first person ever to report on the development of a new country.

His explorations took place during the annual harvest recess, when Dwight would resolutely launch himself from coastal Connecticut into the rough and ready backcountry. Already middle-aged at the start of his journeys, he zestfully took to the frontier's horrid roads on horseback until age sixty, soldiering on in later years by chaise or sulky. When his horse was unable to overcome the mire, New England's most famous minister muddied himself to the knees, occasionally arriving so late at a rude log "tavern" that he had to go to bed hungry.

Of particular concern to Dwight was the economy and character of New Englanders themselves. A sixth generation Yankee, he considered his fellows to be altogether remarkable, exceptionally healthy, and superior to the English in every respect. From our perspective, his view that New Englanders "like strangers in the land, would soon not know the origins of their own rapidly altering society," rings even truer today than it did two hundred years ago.

Let us now cover the footprints of this enthusiastic and memorable wayfarer with tracks of our own. Timothy Dwight, lead on.

Along the Connecticut
Preface to Tours 1-5

TIME AND THE RIVER

A half-billion years of the earth's history are on view between the mouth of the White River and the heights of Newbury, forty miles to the north. The record isn't continuous, but it will do. Admittedly, rocks can be pretty dense material, so you may wish to skip ahead to "Geology for Dummies." No hard feelings if you do.

An old furrow in Father Time's brow, the valley of the Connecticut had its origins in the triple breakup of North America, Eurasia and Africa that began during the Triassic, 200 million years ago. For the previous fifty million years, the ancestral continents had been fused into one landmass: Pangea. Continental drift then split up this ménage à trois, with the individual plates rafting away from one another at two or three inches per year to form today's more familiar map of the world. Major fissures that developed during the divorce became the Amazon, Niger, Mississippi, and lower Connecticut basins. Over the next tens of millions of years, the southern end of the local crevasse filled with dry climate sediments, the type one finds in the American Southwest today. These sediments are exposed as the crumbly and very un-New Englandy red earth seen along I-91 south of Hartford in the Nutmeg State.

Geologists are less certain about the origins of the upper half of the valley, but jointing is the probable explanation. Most likely, blocks of earth moved along faults, with the local Ammonoosuc Fault eventually connecting to the lower basin to form a long downwarp in the earth. As a rugged rift valley, the Connecticut was not unlike that in East Africa today.

As time's arrow flew through the Jurassic of 150 million years ago toward the dino-crazy Cretaceous, the triple disjunction of Pangea continued, and the Atlantic Ocean found a home for itself in between. During the Cretaceous, dinosaurs did their usual roaming in the lower Connecticut basin, leaving their footprints in mud as far north as central Massachusetts.

Compared to the imperceptible creep of the fracturing continents that first formed it, the present soft contours of the valley were fashioned by nature almost instantaneously. One hundred thousand years of glacial advance and retreat have sculpted the valley into the friendly and familiar territory we know so well. After the most recent icy pulse, known as the Wisconsin sheet, a two-hundred-mile-long lake occupied the valley for some thousands of years. Ever since this finger lake drained off, the Connecticut has been lazily cutting its way down through the soft mud of the lake bottom.

Though geologists may be iffy about just how faulting created the Connecticut River Valley, they are supremely confident about the origin of local mountains. In New Hampshire, fracturing deep underground associated with post-Pangean continental drift allowed slurpy magma to rise, elevating the much older "country rock" above. The heavily weathered metamorphic rock on top, rather than the volcanic material below, is known today as the White Mountains. The magma that managed to ooze near enough to the surface to be exposed later became the granite of the Granite State.

Northbound on River Road

This mountain building was of a most unusual kind. At the time the granite was rising 120 million years ago (mya), the North American plate was skimming over a weakness in the earth's mantle—the Great Meteor Hot Spot. In relatively quick succession, over the plate slid, out spurted the magma, and up went the Whites and Mt. Ascutney. In a similar fashion, the Pacific Plate has been sliding over a hot spot on the opposite side of the globe for millions of years—voilà! the Hawaiian island chain.

There are much older rocks around here too. As you explore this province of upper New England, you will see shales and volcanic basalts harking back through incomprehensible depths of time to the 300 mya Silurian and the 400 mya Ordovician eras. They lay differently then but have been squeezed, cooked, twisted, intruded upon, flipped on end and upside down (like home fries on a diner griddle), melted, eroded, redeposited, subducted, and reformatted so many times that making sense of them is a tribulation that will keep geologists schist-deep in grant applications for at least another century.

One other earthshaking event figures into the local surface geology of the valley. Before Pangea there had to be a some-place for our continental plate to be, of course, which was usually on the move crisscrossing the equator. And while it was cruising around, it had to find something to do, so it sparred with other landmasses for position on the surface of the globe. Others were doing the same. About some 450 mya, the then hatchet-shaped eastern North American plate was socked on its right coast by a nimble archipelago of Aleutian-like volcanic islands. Still around today, what is known as the Bronson Hill complex stretches like link sausages from Long Island Sound northeast along the Connecticut to the Maine border. The Lebanon Dome, around which the socially disjuncted tri-towns of Hanover, White River, and Lebanon are arranged, is rock pushed up by the root of one of these volcanic islands. How thoughtfully it was placed there almost half a billion years ago too so that local mountain bikers today wouldn't have to go far to find trails.

After the advancing Bronson Hill volcano necklace was welded onto Vermont's eastern margin, the main body that was driving it showed up—a brawny tectonic plate named Gondwana. Gondwana came in force, closing the Atlantic Ocean and bulldozing all the rocks before it from Alabama to the Gaspé in Quebec into the neat folds known as the Appalachian Mountains. (Pangea had now formed.) When the clinch broke up fifty million years later, an eastwardly retreating Gondwana left a hunk of itself behind, a shoulder stuck onto North America. Today, as the kind of foreign immigrant geopoet John McPhee calls "suspect terrane," this rocky artifact takes in eastern N.H., Downeast Maine, and the Canadian Maritimes.

So if you have even wondered why native Granite Staters and Maine-iacs seem to differ so from other New Englanders at times, now you know. Although most aren't aware of it, these Yankees hail from Africa.

The music of the wind in the trees brought messages floating down millions of years of time.
  William O. Douglas, *Of Men and Mountains*, 1950

GEOLOGY FOR DUMMIES, A 400-MILLION-YEAR-LONG RIDE UP THE CONNECTICUT VALLEY

Before the quiz, let's recap, reviewing the geologic development of the region as though it took place on a 430-million-year-long bicycle ride up the Connecticut from Norwich. Since the Upper Valley lies closer to the equator for much of the period, the ride will be a steamy one. On the other hand, Vermont was flat at the outset, so the pedaling will be easy to start with.

Right from the beginning, the route parallels a chain of volcanic islands known as the Bronsons. You can see them puffing along abreast and offshore to your right, out there in the Iapetus Ocean, where N.H. will one day be. These islands are sailing westbound and will dock with Vermont shortly, just about the time you get to Pompanoosuc. But don't stop at Pompy; East Thetford is only five miles ahead and you have plenty of time. Stop there at Huggett's Mini Mart for a Klondike bar. You have forty million years or so to kill while watching the great continent known as Gondwana barging in from the east behind the Bronsons. Hello, Gondy, good-bye, Iapetus; you've been squeezed dry and driven under.

When you get to Fairlee, go right to the flea market at the old depot. By now the terrain has changed and you're going to need a new bike. The collision of the continents—Gondy, North America and Eurasia (which joined the party out of sight to the north)—has accordioned the plains of Vermont up into high mountains. Fairlee might as well be Everest base camp. Not a mountain biker? Well, then wait fifty million years and erosion will have done its work and the profile of Vermont will be more like the washboard it is today than the Himalayas it once was.

By the time you get to Bradford, the Siamese threesome of Gondy, North America and Eurasia will be on the skids, but their breakup isn't a clean one. Members of the local family of rocks have been kidnapped by departing Eurasia to become Scotland and Wales. And impetuous Gondy has separated her left shoulder and left it behind; let's call it Maine and New Hampshire. On a makeover kick, she has stormed off south, there to change her name to Africa.

From the panoramic overlooks on the Newbury plateau farther along, high mountains can be seen doming up to the northeast, as if a mammoth rock-eating mole were burrowing under them. But the humping-up is thanks to magma squirting out of the earth's molten interior. The New Hampshire mountains are swelling up as liquid rock is being extruded into the crust below them, like raspberry jelly filling a donut.

But with 120 million more years to go before you get home, there will be plenty of time for donuts. On your way back south, an East African–like valley will have rifted open all along the way to your left. Stop and watch for a few eons while remains of the Bronson Islands collapse into this trench, there to be buried by sediments running off the Vermont Himalayas. Later on, just about the time you near the River Rd./Route 5 split in Norwich, the stabilizing rift will offer the newborn Connecticut River a comfortable route to a new ocean, named after the Titan Iapetus's son, Atlas.

Back in the village and with only a hundred thousand years to go before Dan & Whit's general store opens for business, your half-billion-year bike ride is nearing its end. And just in time, for as your wheels begin the last half-turn of your seventy-mile circuit of the eons, you feel Boreas's frozen breath over your shoulder. Wouldn't you know it, the first pulse of the Ice Age. Better put studs on those tires.

GLACIER'S GIFT

We live by the lake, all of us, but don't seem to know it. Named Hitchcock, the two-hundred-mile-long remnant of the last glacier is now mostly dried up. Not only does the Upper Valley live along Lake Hitchcock, its people daily spend almost all their time within its bed—working and sleeping, walking, biking, and driving. The geography of the lake almost entirely defines where human activity takes place around here—period. Even if you live on Thetford Hill or the heights of Randolph Center, you look down on what was a vast lake and cross its sometimes obvious shoreline every day without even knowing it. From the Haverhill Commons, to the Dartmouth Green, to the runways at Lebanon's airport, to the lawn of the VA Hospital, to the Quechee polo field, to the Tunbridge fairgrounds, to the Bradford nine-holer, nothing unites this region more than its most recent geologic iteration. The Connecticut River Valley is one big dry lakebed, with one rather small stream running down the middle.

Besides the valley, in 6000 B.C. Lake Hitchcock submerged the White, Waits, Ompompanoosuc, Ammonoosuc, Mascoma, and lower Ottauquechee Rivers' drainages. Like its siblings, New York's Finger Lakes, it was one of the many frigid children of the most recent glacial advance in the current series, the Wisconsin sheet. The unstoppable march of the ice front climaxed some 12,000 years ago on a line running through Cape Cod, New York City, Buffalo, and Dayton, Ohio. Then the climate warmed, and in the southern Connecticut River Valley, meltwater ponded behind a moraine of debris near Hartford. As the glacier receded north at about 250 feet each summer, the lake followed. After a couple thousand years, wet and wild Lake Hitchcock stretched from New Britain, Conn., up along the rift valley through St. Johnsbury as far north as West Burke, Vt., and Lancaster, N.H.

Named for Amherst College geologist Charles Hitchcock, the lake's great size and depth was a function of the monumental weight of its parent. So massive was the mile-thick ice sheet that the earth's crust had actually been depressed beneath it. This meant northern New England was hardly higher than its southern regions, and the frigid meltwater had nowhere to run off.

Although its shoreline varied, at one point Lake Hitchcock appears to have remained stable for 1,600 or more years, freezing and thawing annually in the slowly moderating climate. When the rock pile that impounded it did give way, the effect was catastrophic. In one instance, the lake's level appears to have dropped ninety or more feet in a few days.

How deep was the water in our backyard during those 1,600 years? The most vivid image was drawn by Dartmouth geologist Richard Lougee, who suggested the inundation would have split the clock face on Dartmouth's Baker Tower. All three valleys of the White River looked like fjords, with embayments extending northwest of Randolph into Braintree, to the Williamstown Gulf in Brookfield, and ten miles north of Chelsea into the town of Washington.

On the east side of the Connecticut a number of separate lakes collected around rotting ice masses, with Gacial Lake Mascoma (GLM) becoming one of the largest. Iceberg-dotted GLM embraced the Mascoma River's present drainage plus Goose Pond and most of the town of Canaan. Bottom line? If you're biking on flat terrain anywhere in the Upper Valley today, eight thousand years ago you were underwater.

KAME AND WENT, ESKER ABOUT IT

Although many glacial features that were once the open-air laboratories of local geologists are now forested over, much is still in plain sight right over the handlebars. Terraces along the Connecticut are the most obvious. West Lebanon, for instance, is built on six different lake floor terraces. Other flat features are kame terraces, delta-like deposits that formed on the edges of meltwater lakes surrounding tongues of retreating ice. Differentiating them from lakebeds is graduate-level work though, so it's probably easier to look for a close cousin, the esker.

Halfpipes of sand deposited in tunnels under the ice, eskers run up and down the valleys by the mile, notably for twenty-four miles from Windsor to Thetford. Washed away at Wilder by the down-cutting Connecticut, the esker shows up again in Hanover as River Ridge and Occom Ridge. After visiting these better neighborhoods and giving Chieftain Motor Inn guests an elevated view of Dartmouth crew races, the esker crosses back to the Vermont side. There its deposits are actively mined at several quarries along Route 5. One of these is particularly obvious from I-91, just south of the Ompompanoosuc crossing. If you're a regular biker on Route 5 north of Norwich, you probably have cursed all that sand and gravel you have to continually detour around near the bible church. That's esker falling out of overfilled dump trucks.

Another hundred-foot-high hunk of esker nicely exposes itself along the White River two and a half miles north of Sharon, just a few yards off Route 14. Nearby lies another extraordinary glacial feature—a sandpit with exposures of a thousand years of layered deposits called varves. These lamina record each season of Lake Hitchcock's long history. See both on Tour 35.

Spanning the Ages

A series of memorable bridges nicely segment bicycle rides upriver from Hanover/Norwich into roundtrip tours of 20, 14, 16, and 15 miles long. Thanks to historic preservation laws, four of the spans have been thoughtfully refurbished in recent years, with a fifth, the Ledyard Bridge, replacing a narrow 1930s structure of no great architectural value. South to north, they are:

Ledyard Bridge. The sixth bridge at this location since 1796 and the third to be named for eighteenth-century Dartmouth dropout and world explorer John Ledyard. Pre–Civil War versions were hated monopolies operated by Boston investors. No wonder fractious students returning to nominally dry Hanover from the taverns of Norwich set fire to the privately owned structure in August 1854. Public officials caught their drift and a free bridge followed.

The latest Ledyard Bridge iteration is as controversial as most of its predecessor crossings. Its appearance has been a popular letters-to-the-editor topic since sketches of the arresting cup-and-ball garniture were revealed in the mid-1990s. Love it or loath it, the story of its architecture has much to do with Dartmouth College's calculated disinterest in the look of the bridge during the design phase. But that's a story for another day.

On balance, however, most eyes favor the new bridge's treatment. Those who don't should know that the architect (who was given the job in the eleventh hour) meant for his work to be seen from the river itself, as you will do from River Road in Norwich at the end of Tour 1.

Thetford–Lyme. A short-span, steel-truss bridge, c. 1940, of which America once had thousands. Simple and straightforward, this honest span is to be overhauled by 2010.

Fairlee–Orford. A dazzling gemstone in the Connecticut River's sinuous necklace, the 1938 F-O arched bridge was destined for greatness, thanks to its original conception: "It should be a steel bridge of the very best construction possible. It must be strong, safe, and sightly, a bridge of beauty and utility, fitting accurately into its scenic environment." Restoration of this National Historic Register masterpiece was completed in 2003.

Bradford–Piermont. Another short-span truss form, this recently restored bridge reveals itself most dramatically on the approach from the Vermont side. The working dairy farm on the opposite shore highlights a country scene difficult to believe still exists.

Connecticut River bridge at Bradford-Piermont

Haverhill–Newbury. An off-the-shelf design that accomplishes two things: gets us to the other side and attests to the (ongoing) absence of aesthetic values at the N.H. Dept. of Transportation. To them, beauty is a sign of weakness.

Wells River–Woodsville. While the iron-filigreed auto bridge is more picturesque than ever, the unusual two-level railroad bridge just upstream is of more historic interest. Beginning in the 1850s, wood-powered trains of the *Boston, Concord & Montreal RR* ran on top (see Tour 11), while horse-drawn traffic was conveyed inside a fully enclosed lower level—on a toll-paying basis, of course. Defunct in recent years, the rail bridge's upper level was put into temporary use in 2002 as a detour while its downstream neighbor was being rebuilt.

① Quinnitukut, The Long River
Hanover-East Thetford

To the Abenaki Indians, it was Quinnitukut, the "long river." They gave thanks to the Great Spirit for it because, unlike the rocky White, Quinnitukut had enough water in it to float their canoes. To Dutchman Adriaen Bloch, who tried to be the first European to navigate it in 1614, water levels weren't a concern. The complicating issue, as he learned at the first cataract, was the Connecticut was not always flat. Stymied by the falls at what is now Enfield, Conn., Bloch came about and sailed his small ship back to Long Island Sound.

When Europeans began to settle the Upper Connecticut River Valley a hundred fifty years later, freshwater mariners managed to sail square-rigged flatboats far upriver, poling in the shallows when the prevailing southwest breeze gave out. Known to settlers as the Conicut, the river was western New England's main street. Salt, glass, raw metal, millstones, pottery, cloth, tobacco, and dried fish were transported up it, all laboriously unloaded and reloaded at every falls. Wheat, potash, livestock, maple sugar, and wood products on their way to England and the Caribbean moved downstream in similar fashion. A trip north to the mouth of the White River from Springfield, Mass., might take almost three weeks, but less than half that on the downstream return.

Over the years, canals and locks bypassed a number of cataracts, including the one at Wilder, but the journey was never easy. The trade was valuable enough, though, that coastal Connecticut and New Hampshire interests fought over it. After turnpikes from the Upper Valley to Portsmouth and Boston were opened, Hartford traders attempted to send a small steamboat past Bellows Falls to the upper river. Riding high water in June 1831, the little *Ledyard*—as in Ledyard Bridge—made her way to the mouth of the Ammonoosuc at Wells River/Woodsville. Then it beached on a sandbar. As predicted by the jolly flatboatmen, the long river had proved to be a stream with too little water in it for year-round navigation. Thoreau himself noted this shortcoming in 1850 while out on his very first train ride. "I was disappointed with the size of the river here [Bellows Falls]; it appeared shrunk to a mere mountain stream. The water was evidently very low."

Within a few years, railroads made the Connecticut's carrying capacity moot. Seasonal boat traffic dried up, opening the river, ironically, to industries that would profoundly poison it. Without shipping in the way, spring log drives were now possible, resulting in the founding of pulp and paper mills wherever a falls could be dammed for the power to drive them.

In this next phase of the Connecticut's history, the river went from a favorite scene of Hudson River School artists to "the best landscaped sewer in the world." For over a century, caustic wastes from paper, wool, tanning, metal forming, and a hundred other industries were flushed directly into the river, to be mixed with sewage and rubbish thrown over the bank from every town along the way. The Connecticut's tributaries were treated no better, with one historian noting the color of cloth being made at Enfield's Baltic Mill on any one day could be known by just looking at the Mascoma as it flowed through town to the lake. In downtown Lebanon, a tannery used the Mascoma as a handy dump for huge gobs of acid-laced horsehair when the material could no longer be sold as plaster filler.

How bad was it? In a collection of oral histories of life on the Connecticut, gathered in the 1990s by Suzanne Nothnagel, one recollection of those foul times is exceptionally vivid: "My Dad and I used to put a canoe in up by the golf course in Bradford, paddle out to the [mouth of] the Waits River and go in there and hunt. I'd see these strange things hanging in bushes that only later I realized were condoms."

These reveries may not encourage one to drink river water, even thirty years after cleanup began. But how about topical application; can you swim in the Connecticut today? Absolutely. Today Quinnitukut is a long, pretty, clean river. A notable occasion for a baptism in its waters occurs in mid July at the Dartmouth student–sponsored hoot called Tubestock. Be there in a black rubber toroid or be square.

Point of View

Springing from a mountain pool and highland rivulets . . . the Connecticut winds and curves and bows its gracious way three hundred sixty miles to the sea. The Valley's charm is found in the frequency and magnitude of the fertile meadows . . . and the processions of splendid terraces rising between intervening glens.

Edwin M. Bacon, *The Connecticut River*, 1907

East Thetford Road, Lyme

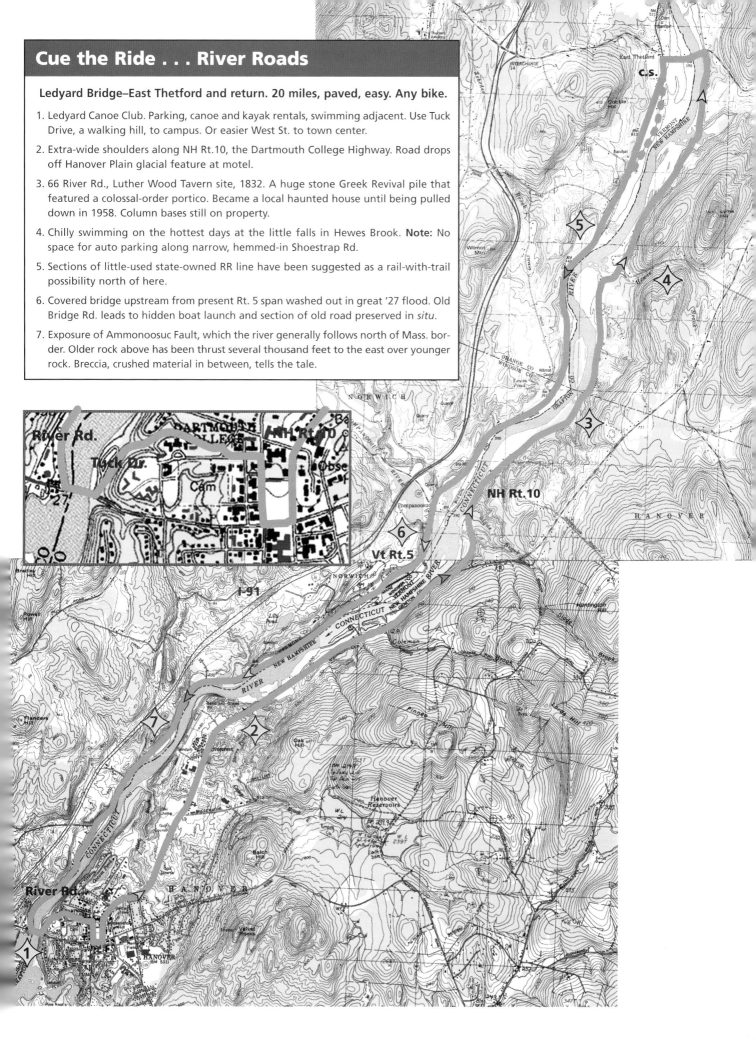

Cue the Ride . . . River Roads

Ledyard Bridge–East Thetford and return. 20 miles, paved, easy. Any bike.

1. Ledyard Canoe Club. Parking, canoe and kayak rentals, swimming adjacent. Use Tuck Drive, a walking hill, to campus. Or easier West St. to town center.

2. Extra-wide shoulders along NH Rt.10, the Dartmouth College Highway. Road drops off Hanover Plain glacial feature at motel.

3. 66 River Rd., Luther Wood Tavern site, 1832. A huge stone Greek Revival pile that featured a colossal-order portico. Became a local haunted house until being pulled down in 1958. Column bases still on property.

4. Chilly swimming on the hottest days at the little falls in Hewes Brook. **Note:** No space for auto parking along narrow, hemmed-in Shoestrap Rd.

5. Sections of little-used state-owned RR line have been suggested as a rail-with-trail possibility north of here.

6. Covered bridge upstream from present Rt. 5 span washed out in great '27 flood. Old Bridge Rd. leads to hidden boat launch and section of old road preserved in *situ*.

7. Exposure of Ammonoosuc Fault, which the river generally follows north of Mass. border. Older rock above has been thrust several thousand feet to the east over younger rock. Breccia, crushed material in between, tells the tale.

2 Taverns and Tack

Thetford-Orford

tour continued on next page

Cue the Ride . . . Taverns & Tack

East Thetford–Orford and return.
16 miles, easy/moderate. Any bike.

Travel north along the old stagecoach route to Orford, then across the restored arched bridge to Fairlee. Power up with a lobster roll at the storied Fairlee Diner for two major hills on the VT Rt.5 return.

1. First brick house was Green Tavern, 1771. Washboard transition to hard dirt section ahead.

2. Three Beavers Tavern, 1780s. St. Francis "Indian" parents from Quebec stayed here while visiting their sons at Dartmouth. Most weren't Native Americans at all, but white men, descendants of captives taken to Canada in raids before 1750.

3. Decrepit bridge to North Thetford removed, 1970s. A footbridge replacement would be a great idea, as long as the white birch growing out of the old mid-river abutment isn't troubled.

4. Use caution on steep descent to blind approach at covered bridge over Clay Brook. Stream is named for the soft Lake Hitchcock sediments that it has cut through en route to the river.

5. Site of massive Houghton's Pavilion Stock Barn, with stalls for 200 harness horses on four floors, built by Boston dept. store owner in 1877. The 130-foot tower had four clock faces, huge bell. Tower fell 1920s, barn later burned. Curve of racetrack still visible.

6. Road cut along interstate exposes slates from lower Devonian, 450 mya. Local region was then sea bottom near the equator.

7. Ely depot. Until WWI, shipping point for concentrated copper ore from Ely Mine, Vershire. See Tour 26.

8. Childs Pond. Kettle holes like this one are formed by blocks of silt-entombed ice that survive the melting of the parent glacier.

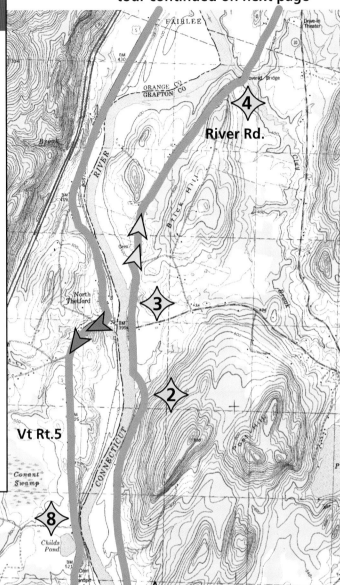

Lake Morey

Point of View

Of Lyme, the township above Hanover, we saw very little, as the road passes along the foot of the hills and very near the river. The journey was, however, pleasant and romantic, the river, bordered in several places by small intervals, being frequently in sight and forming a cheerful contrast to the solemnity of the forest.

Timothy Dwight, *Journey to the White Mountains*, Letter X, Sept. 28, 1797

③ Samuel Morey, Giant Among Men
Fairlee

Samuel Morey, a mechanical genius from Orford, made only one mistake in his life, but it cost him big. Although his first invention, a steam-powered spit to turn meat, was modest, he knew the ins and outs of the patent business well, or should have. Around 1800 Morey began to apply steam to the problem of propulsion, rigging a small boiler and engine in a dugout canoe just big enough to carry the machinery, some firewood, and him. The engine turned a small paddlewheel at the bow with sufficient force to pull the boat up the Connecticut River at five miles an hour. Eureka! He had invented the "steam boat."

After developing a larger, improved version of the affair, Morey filed for a patent. Later he took the rig to New York to demonstrate it to an investment syndicate. Others were working on powered watercraft at the time, including a fellow named Robert Fulton. Fulton noticed Morey's patent drawings failed to include what turned out to be the *sine qua non* of the invention—twin paddlewheels. End of story. So forgotten is the steamboat's real inventor that some biographies of Fulton don't even mention Morey.

Swallowing his pride, Samuel Morey went on to gain twenty more patents, including one for which historians—of science, at least—celebrate his genius. He mixed steam with volatile vapors, such as turpentine, in ominous experiments in his barn. In 1826 his "explosive engine," complete with valved cylinder, crankshaft, and flywheel, was granted a patent. This was surely the first internal combustion engine ever made. And not only did he design a model, three years later he was *motoring* on the lake that now bears his name at the helm of a nineteen-foot gas engine boat. This, a half-century before Daimler developed the next working example in Germany. Morey even experimented with electric ignition for the engine.

Samuel Morey took out his last patent in 1833 at age 71. His prediction that "loco-motive engines" would power transport over rails or on good roads with "little use of horses" was entirely accurate. Unfortunately, although a model of his unique and revolutionary internal combustion engine can be seen in Washington, his contributions to science and mechanics are almost entirely unknown outside the local area.

In the 1870s, the Vermont Historical Society investigated claims by an old coot that he had watched Morey's gas boat—a red and white number named *Aunt Sally*—sink at the north end of the lake. Searchers probing the water with grappling hooks turned up nothing.

Giant Steps . . . 1 Bike Ride, 2 Hikes

Lake Morey Loop. 5 miles, easy. Any bike. No cues needed.
Two short, steep, and highly rewarding hikes are noted instead.

Squeezed in between the hard rocks of Echo Mountain and the Palisade, the Wisconsin ice sheet could only rout out a channel in between, leaving behind a cleft for Lake Morey to fill. Dazzling now when seen from promontories above—almost as though from an airplane—the lake appears as if a giant has scooped it out for a drinking cup.

Lake Morey Hiking Trails

1. Palisade Trail, white blazes. Begins inside fence at very end of interstate off-ramp, adjacent to rescue squad building. Through the peregrine falcon nesting season, ending July 30, the short, steep trail can be climbed to views from power lines only. After that date, continue on 10 mins. to village overlook from the precipice.

2. Echo Mt. and Bald Top Trails. Both begin opposite boat ramp on the west shore. The Echo Mt. loop, returning by road from north end of lake, takes 1.5 hrs. Steep up, easier down. The new trail to panoramic views from Bald Top (3 hrs. roundtrip) will become a section of the in-development Cross Rivendell Trail, running east–west from Mt. Cube in Orford to Flagpole Hill, Vershire.

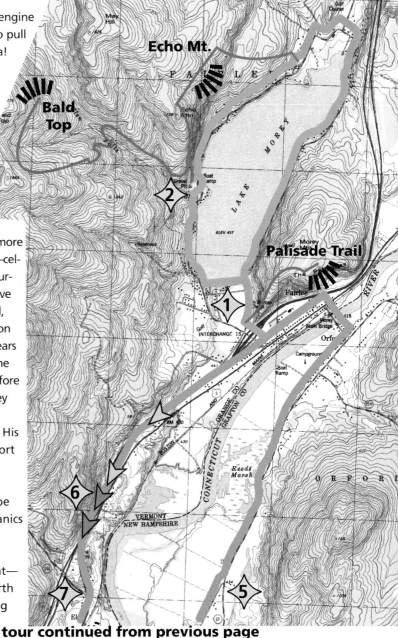

tour continued from previous page

4 Great Leap Northward 🚲
Orford-Bradford

In the 1740s, land in the Upper Valley sold for 30 cents an acre, but there was little market for it without assurance of protection from the Indians in Quebec. And for good reason. Over the previous half century, the Connecticut River Valley had been the preferred invasion route of Abenaki raiding parties, with Deerfield in the western Massachusetts Bay Colony a frequent target.

After an attack in April 1704, some of the 106 English settlers kidnapped from Deerfield were held prisoner in makeshift camps near the mouths of the Waits and Wells Rivers in what are now Bradford and Newbury. Their jailers, mostly women, were preparing to put in crops of corn and pumpkins in the oxbow of the Connecticut flood plain nearby. Later that summer, several other provincials taken captive in northeastern Massachusetts joined this odd assemblage. These new unfortunates had been driven north through New Hampshire along the Pemigewasset and Baker Rivers' drainages, along a route that would later become the Coos (*Coe-OSS*) Turnpike.

Years afterward, when some of the English were ransomed from Canada, they took back with them firsthand news of the wealth of the Indian gardens of the Coos. Tales of the alluvial El Dorado grew, and fifty years later, just as soon as the French and Indians had been defeated on the Plains of Abraham below Quebec City, whites hurried back north. The first to arrive were surveyors Bayley and Hazen, who grabbed off pieces of the choicest townships for themselves in exchange for services rendered to N.H. colonial governor Benning Wentworth. Along with their surveying equipment, the two took with them the names of their hometowns, Newbury and Haverhill, which adjoined one another on the Merrimack River in the Massachusetts Bay Colony.

In 1760, with his choicest holdings now dispersed to the Mass. men, Governor Wentworth in Portsmouth moved quickly to refresh his inventory. Surveyors dispatched to the dark pine woods south of the Coos carried 16.5-foot measuring chains—the "rod"—and instructions to lay out townships on either side of the river, six miles on a side. (The rod measures 16.5 feet. Multiply that times 32 and you get 5,280 feet, so the rod is not so clumsy a length to work with after all.) Local towns in what would later become Vermont were drawn off "a white pine opposite the SW corner of Lebanon across the Connicut River." This haphazard accommodation of spyglass geography assured a cacophony of claims and counterclaims that would take land courts more than a century to unsnarl. And since the countryside was all New Hampshire then, litigation over where the border itself was ended up in the Supreme Court. The Granite State won the battle and owns the Connecticut. What it got besides the privilege of paying for the bridges is not known.

With newly drawn township plats from the surveyors in hand and with 500 acres for himself in mind, Wentworth reached for his goose quill early and often the next summer. Among other towns, he chartered Hartford, Woodstock, Pomfret, Barnard, Sharon, Lebanon, Hanover, Enfield, and Lyme, many of them, prophetically, on July 4. A land rush known as the "Great Swarming" was on, impelled by raring-to-go downcountry development syndicates.

Regardless of Massachusetts-originated Haverhill and Newbury, the early Upper Valley was all about Connecticut. Each spring, beginning in the 1760s, men walked up along the *Connecticut* River from the *Connecticut* colony to new townships all named after locations in *Connecticut*. Others rode horses along the banks, and a few canoed, most spending the summer living in a bough hut while girdling and chopping the forest primeval. When the slash had dried, it was put to the torch, nourishing the soil with potash. Unless they ran out of supplies like salt, these axe men kept expanding their clearings until November, when they cached their tools in the woods and went home—to *Connecticut*. Not surprisingly, when, twenty years later, a move to unite towns on both sides of the river into a separate political entity arose, the proposed state was to be called New *Connecticut*.

In Norwich the first clearing was made in 1763 on a bench above the Ompompanoosuc. Two years later, Thetford's first permanent resident, Quail John Chamberlain, wintered all alone nearby. Pomfret got going in a big way in 1770 when a crew of nineteen began to hack a road north through the woods from the Ottauquechee, a track that survives as Hillside Road and Spalding Lane (Tour 32). Woodstock was slightly ahead of Pomfret, having already been civilized by Timothy Knox, a reclusive Harvard man who put a basswood roof over his head along the Kedron Brook. (Harvard? Seems like it should have been Princeton or Williams.) Up country, Randolph didn't see permanent settlement until after Paul Revere's ride.

The women and children and a cow followed the woodcutters the second to the fourth years, sometimes just for the summer. Wheat was planted among the stumps, a mill site was located to grind it, and that was that. When the French millstones were hauled up over the ice by oxen the next winter, the wilderness was tamed. Now our forefathers could get on with a century and a half of what town histories indicate really interested them—endless parsing of which narrow slice of Protestant dogma should dominate their untidy corner of New Paradise.

Cue the Ride . . . Great Leap

Orford–Piermont–Bradford Lower Plain & return. 14 miles, easy. Any bike. Counterclockwise ride may be more scenic, if that were possible.

1. NH Rt.10. Easy grades, little traffic. Shoulder widens at Piermont line.

2. Glorious river panorama from behind elementary school.

3. Carnival of pumpkins, October.

4. Dairy lands. Explore sideroads.

5. Sawyer Mt., actual "falling rock zone."

6. Unique Fairlee Drive-In Theatre and Motel, seemingly always for sale, just sold, or about to go on the market. Allée of locust trees and granite fence posts ahead lead into town. Good eats at the first place on your left.

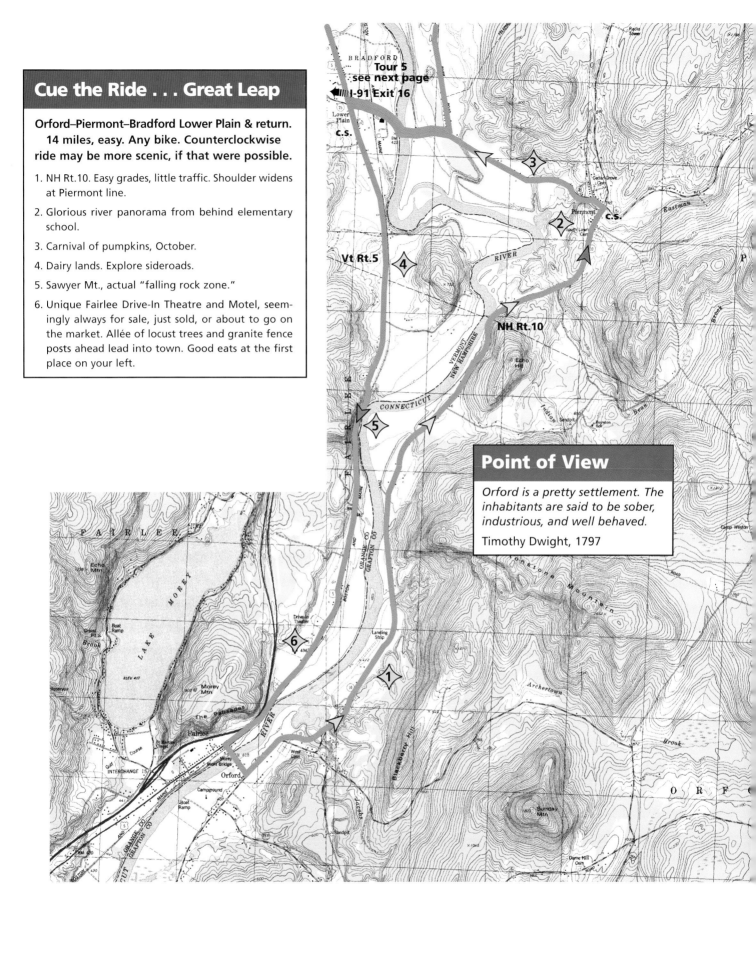

Point of View

Orford is a pretty settlement. The inhabitants are said to be sober, industrious, and well behaved.

Timothy Dwight, 1797

5 Along the Turnpikes 🚲
Bradford-Newbury

Few people seem to know that hundreds of miles of New England roads now used by bicycles and cars originally were built as privately owned businesses—turnpikes. Today these country avenues look just like every other road and go unrecognized, even if the sign at the corner says Turnpike Road. Tollbooths—their only above-ground artifacts—have been recycled long since, with the few survivors rarely identified for the enjoyment of passersby. Here and there, though, abandoned sections of the old toll roads still speak of the ox drovers, peddlers, and itinerant artists from the days of Madison, Monroe, Adams (John Q.), and Jackson.

Two hundred years ago, turnpike schemes were the dot.coms of the day, with forty-seven companies chartered in N.H. in the first decade of the 1800s. Chartering meant a private company enjoyed the right to take land along whatever route it chose, usually in exchange for stock. After a route was surveyed, road builders were sent out with broad axes to have at the giants of the wilderness. Like systems engineers at 1990s startups, the surveyors and tree cutters were paid partially in paper—IPO shares that usually held the most value before the turnpike opened. When complete, the projects cost the developers one to five thousand dollars a mile, depending on the terrain.

As contemporary bikers soon learn, turnpike surveyors didn't often follow the path of least resistance, often plowing up over the dry hills in as straight a line as possible. Trees were felled and brush was cut to a width of three rods, a limb was trimmed for a tollgate, and the ribbon was snipped. At first, rocks, roots, stumps, and swamps along the way were the travelers' problem, not the developer's. Money-making main drags, however, were soon able to raise centerlines for better drainage and use tree-branch graders to fill potholes. Neglect was more often the case, but at least the law allowed State turnpike inspectors to throw open the tollgates if the road became impassable.

At the outset, these rude creations were the best thoroughfares around, designed and built for teamsters and drovers as a kind of early truck route. Typically, turnpike companies charged a penny a mile for a horse and rider, and two cents a mile for each ten cattle being driven to market. Toll roads were not for everyday use by local people though. Country folk rarely traveled far before the advent of railroads, having little occasion to leave their own neighborhoods. During sleighing season, casual traffic could be heavy, as more prosperous upcountry farmers from the region headed south toward markets in the new mill city of Lowell, Mass. If the snow was good, folks with butter and brown sugar to sell might continue on to the city market at Cambridge, where prices were higher.

The first of these regional ventures, the Coos Turnpike, was hacked out of the wilderness from the Baker River near Warren, N.H., northwest to the Connecticut River Valley in 1804. Haverhill, on the river, instantly became the most important town between Concord and Montreal. Begun as a crude haul road, the Coos Turnpike soon became the final link in what was the Interstate 89 of the day. As a combination freeway and toll road via Plymouth and Portsmouth, it carried wheat and produce from the bottomlands, known as the Coos, to the Boston markets, washouts and mud permitting. The fancy architecture of Haverhill testifies to its success. Built and rebuilt over the next fifty years, some of the turnpike's stone bridge piers remained in use by auto traffic into the 1930s.

Unlike the Coos, most turnpike schemes failed to attract enough business to make a profit. Many that were chartered were never able to peddle enough stock (or sell enough lottery tickets) to chop the first tree. But those that served the needs of the wilderness tamers still cover the map, unrecognized and unimagined, as though the roads we drive on today were built for Model T buyers to have someplace to exercise their machines. As late as 1917, four privately owned turnpikes were still operating in New Hampshire and one in Vermont—several as "carriage roads" to mountaintops, as in the "This Car Climbed Mt. Washington" bumper stickers. Surprisingly, one private toll bridge over the Connecticut, between Springfield and Charlestown, survived into the first months of the twenty-first century.

The Oxbow and
Mt. Moosilauke, Newbury

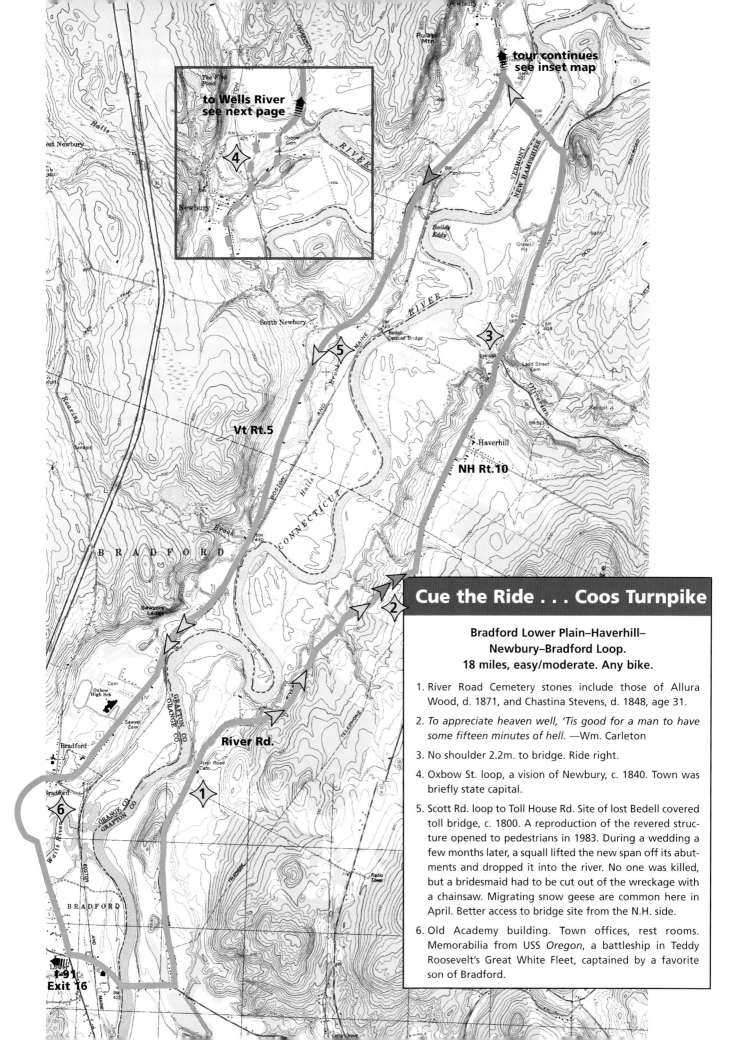

to Wells River
see next page

tour continues
see inset map

Cue the Ride . . . Coos Turnpike

**Bradford Lower Plain–Haverhill–
Newbury–Bradford Loop.
18 miles, easy/moderate. Any bike.**

1. River Road Cemetery stones include those of Allura Wood, d. 1871, and Chastina Stevens, d. 1848, age 31.

2. *To appreciate heaven well, 'Tis good for a man to have some fifteen minutes of hell.* —Wm. Carleton

3. No shoulder 2.2m. to bridge. Ride right.

4. Oxbow St. loop, a vision of Newbury, c. 1840. Town was briefly state capital.

5. Scott Rd. loop to Toll House Rd. Site of lost Bedell covered toll bridge, c. 1800. A reproduction of the revered structure opened to pedestrians in 1983. During a wedding a few months later, a squall lifted the new span off its abutments and dropped it into the river. No one was killed, but a bridesmaid had to be cut out of the wreckage with a chainsaw. Migrating snow geese are common here in April. Better access to bridge site from the N.H. side.

6. Old Academy building. Town offices, rest rooms. Memorabilia from USS *Oregon*, a battleship in Teddy Roosevelt's Great White Fleet, captained by a favorite son of Bradford.

Vt Rt.5

NH Rt.10

River Rd.

I-91
Exit 16

Point of View

The next morning we left Bath and rode to the ferry at Orford, through Newbury, Bradford, and Fairlee, all in Vermont. The river here is perhaps twenty-five rods in breadth, deep and of a brisk current. The boat was managed [at Newbury] by two children, smaller than I have ever seen trusted with such an employment. Immediately below the ferry lies a remarkable interval, extensively known in New England by the name of the Great Oxbow, and still more extensively by the name of the Lower Coos. The whole extent is one vast meadow, covered with the richest verdure, except a small tract covered by arable ground; and it is scarcely possible for mere earth to exhibit a more beautiful surface.

Timothy Dwight, *Journey to the Canada Line*, Letter IX, Oct. 1803

Blackmount Railtrail ▬ ▬ ▬ ▬

After snowmobile season, miles of abandoned rail corridor along the Boston & Maine's old Blackmount section go unnoticed and unridden between North Haverhill and Woodsville. At its southern end, the scenic trail begins in a cornfield along NH Rt.10 near Brier Hill Rd., ending four miles away in the artifact-filled Horse Meadow railyards. Adventurous railroad buffs can also track the railbed south toward Haverhill proper, using the adjoining map and Tour 11 to chart a route. Follow clues from the old depot in North Haverhill along a local street that was once the ROW, then be on the lookout for a massive granite viaduct inexplicably emerging from the woods into a farm field.

A few miles later the cinder-covered trail arrives in Haverhill near Ladd St., having suffered erosion, cratering and obstruction along the way.

This photo looks south from just above North Haverhill. May buttercups in the valley, traces of a late season snowfall on Mt. Moosilauke—an Upper Valley spring.

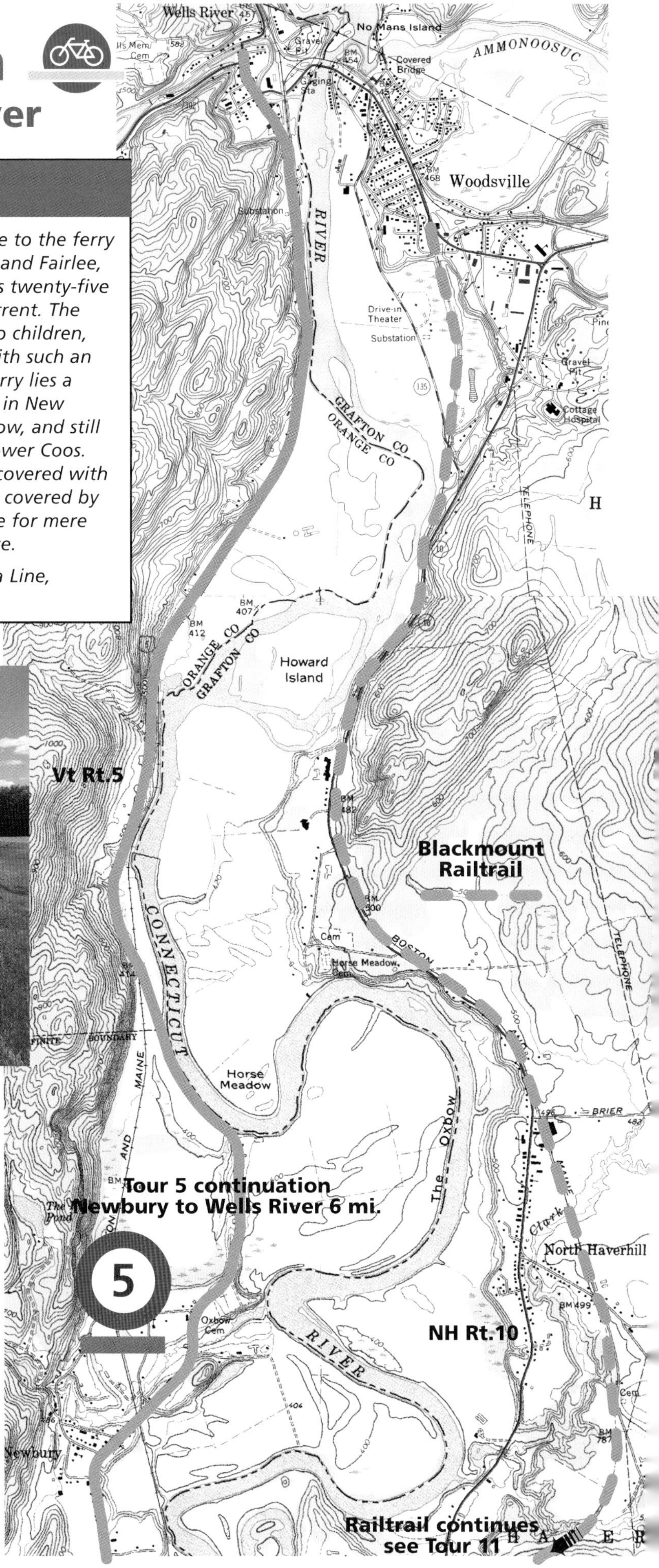

Vt Rt.5

Blackmount Railtrail

Tour 5 continuation Newbury to Wells River 6 mi.

⑤

NH Rt.10

Railtrail continues see Tour 11

Upper Valley Railtrails
Preface to Tours 6-11

Railtrails are as basic to New Biking as air is to tires; neither is going much of anywhere without plenty of the other. These dedicated pathways are the entry points for the sport, where hopeful New Bikers first become enthused. Yet somehow or other, railtrails still require explanation—if not justification—as a legitimate recreational venue. Once a railroad, always a railroad, it seems. But since we need to suit up and get outside where we belong, there's no time right now for the why, only the what and where of these bike paths from heaven.

New Hampshire and Vermont railtrails vary greatly in surface finish and "bikeability," as do trails elsewhere in the U.S. and Europe. And, similar to others, ours enjoy the two attributes that make biking and walking them particularly rewarding: beauty and modesty of grade. Here again geography is destiny. In the East, rail corridors invariably followed watercourses, hence their beauty. And whether built in the East or the West, railways had to be engineered on a slope no greater than 2 percent or they were destined for high operating costs and probable failure. The heritage of these gentle gradients are the scenic embankments, rock cuts, tunnels, and high bridges that add visual excitement to railtrail riding today. Railtrails—beauteous, flat, and tellers of nineteenth-century tales in stone and steel. No wonder they are the birthplace of New Bikers.

From a riding perspective, there are two species of railtrails—as different as cats and dogs—with many sub-category breeds therein. Formal trails—the cats—are those disused rail corridors purposely redeveloped for recreation. Invariably state owned, these bikeways usually arise from post-1990 abandonment. One example is the Northern Railtrail (Tours 7 & 8), which local volunteer orgs cleared of ties and resurfaced for bicycle use at the turn of the century. Informal trails—the dogs—trace much older discontinuances. These rail corridors were appropriated for recreation on the fly, often many years later and usually by snowmobilers. As mongrels, these nameless railtrails can also function as private driveways, town roads, parking lots, or quarries.

In northern New England, a third interspecies version sometimes occurs. The Cross Vermont Trail (Tours 9 & 10), which uses the Montpelier & Wells River line east of Montpelier (RIP 1956), includes a menagerie of both formal and informal sections. When community activists discovered its bicycling potential in the mid '90s, they soon noticed that over forty years, the M&WR's right of way had been parted out—chunks sold off, built on, hauled away, and paved over. Humpty Dumpty would have to be put back together again. Similarly, re-creating New Hampshire's Oliverian Branch (Tour 11 and opposite) as a four-season through-trail will also mean painful reassembly. Such efforts usually become a difficult land-use task, given that abutters often imagine the land under the tracks reverted to them once the railroad wheezed its last.

WHITE RIVER JUNCTION.: RAILTRAIL METROPOLIS 2015?

Today, Upper Valley railtrails might be rated fair and steadily improving. But future prospects are nothing short of spectacular. Railtrail boosters currently are salivating over a diamond in the rough—the Connecticut River rail line between White River Jct. and Wells River (forty miles to the north), which Vermont purchased out of bankruptcy in 2003. Not only would a "Great Riverway Trail" along the mother river be one of the most scenic in the world, it would function as the keystone of a northern New England system of major trails. Furthermore, two conceptual long-distance corridors would be united: the north/south Boston-Manchester-Concord-Lebanon-White River Jct. axis (to include the Northern Railtrail), and the east/west Portland-Gorham-Littleton-Woodsville/Wells River-Montpelier-Burlington axis. Segments of both currently are being made bikeable under a variety of names. A link between the two would put downtown White River Jct. right back where it was a century ago—full of expectant travelers on their way to everywhere.

A non-railtrail—Tour 6 between Woodstock and Quechee—is included in this section as a special case because it too arose directly from railway abandonment. Until 1933, the Woodstock Railroad operated between Woodstock and White River Jct. over a sweeping right of way that is now U.S. Route 4. A high-polish short line, the railroad had been financed in the 1870s by Woodstock's Gilded Age wealthy to connect White River Jct. with points south, mainly Grand Central Station. Once the WRR's directors threw in the towel during the Great Depression, the state immediately appropriated what was a ready-to-roll auto route. Up went the rails and ties; down went the asphalt, including atop the railroad bridge that spanned Quechee Gorge. This relocation has left winding River Road, on the opposite bank of the Ottauquechee River, wide open for easy cycling ever since. Goodbye, Packards and Hupmobiles; hello, petite Tour de France en famille.

Northern Railtrail
October outing along the
Mascoma River, Lebanon

6 Quechee Falls 🚴

Schussing its way down from Killington into the valley below, the Ottauquechee is still a little river by the time it lazes its way onto the flats around Woodstock. Southerners might even call it a creek, but its languor is deceptive. In November 1927, it swelled to the one-hundred-year flood stage, swatting away seven covered bridges along Route 4 between Bridgewater and Woodstock alone.

But what power surge could the same small river possibly have harnessed to slice into bedrock and cut a gorge over a hundred feet deep farther downstream at Quechee? Certainly, ten thousand years ago, Noah-sized volumes of water were available from melting ice rather than the sky, but this doesn't quite explain how Vermont came to have the remains of a fresh wound across its mid-section. To explain, we turn to local geology text-book author David Laing.

According to Laing, before the Ice Age, the Ottauquechee ran more to the east, through the present trailer park just off Route 4. As the icecap melted, a morainal hill of sand filled the old channel and directed the river's course a half-mile to the west, where it runs today. In this period of

Cue the Ride . . . Quechee Falls

Woodstock–Quechee Gorge and return. 17 miles, easy, scenic.

After the Woodstock to White River railroad sounded its last whistle in 1933, Route 4 was quickly removed to its roadbed, leaving an "old road" behind. And what a friendly old road it is, probably the most popular bicycle route in the area for visitors today. Although the suggested route is to Quechee Gorge from Woodstock, direction doesn't matter. Note: Without shoulders, US Rt.4 between Woodstock and Quechee IS TO BE AVOIDED AT ALL TIMES. The short stretch between the gorge and the blinker light at Quechee Village offers two-foot shoulders where cyclists can feel somewhat comfortable.

1. Billings Farm, a must see. Top-drawer interpretation of how the gentry idealized farming before WWI. National Park Service tours of the adjacent mansion and estate are equally first rate.

2. Daniel Taft dammed the river here for mills around 1800; also built most of the period homes in the village. Later, town lines were rearranged so that the entire covered bridge sits in Taftsville (Woodstock) and none in Quechee (Hartford).

3. Quechee Lakes second-home development, once sued by Conn. consumer affairs for misrepresenting "lakes" when there was only one (and that one artificial). Plastic bottom keeps water in.

4. Simon Pearce glass works, another must. See display of period dynamo in lower level. Covered bridge adjacent is ordinary steel structure with a 1960s hat on it.

5. Path from overlook on east end of bridge leads down into mouth of the gorge. Little-known path on west side leads upstream to falls and mill site, connects to lavish avian display at Vermont Institute of Natural Science complex (2004/5).

fluctuating warmth, the Ott behaved less like a free-flowing river and more like a narrow back bay of Lake Hitchcock, the mighty glacial lake that overlay nearly all of what is now the Connecticut and its major tributaries. When the debris that held back the lake broke and Hitchcock drained cataclysmically, a waterfall began to migrate quickly up the lake's muddy bottom from New Britain, Conn., northward. The waterfall bifurcated each time it reached an upstream tributary like the Ott, which it met at North Hartland. After effortlessly washing out four miles of soft mud from the Connecticut to Quechee, the cataract ran up against a formation of bedrock schist and stopped dead. Its cutting was slowed to an imperceptible creep, not unlike the upstream advance of the falls on the Niagara River today.

continues ⫸

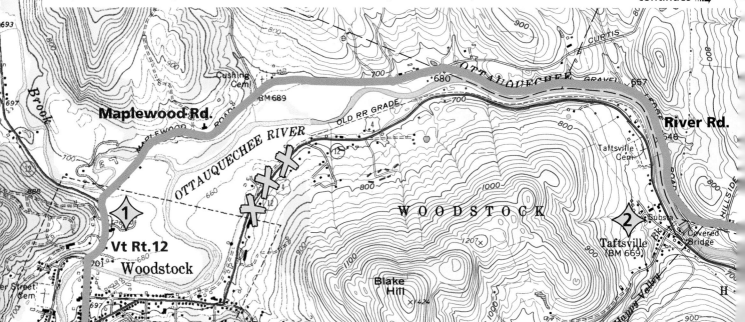

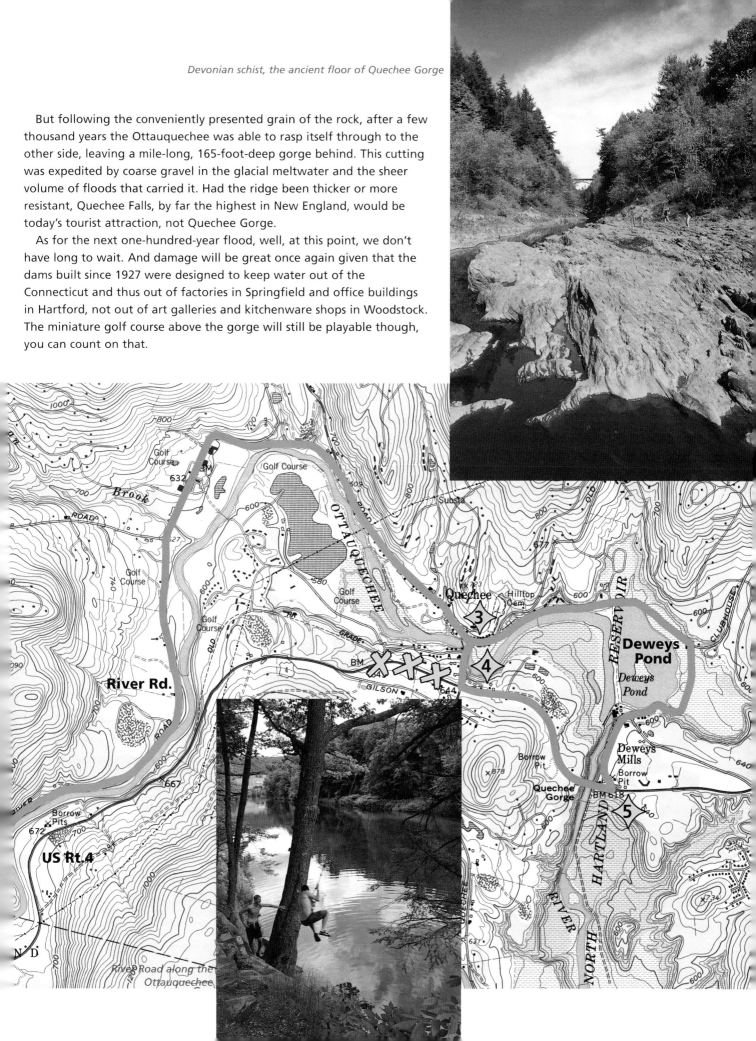

Devonian schist, the ancient floor of Quechee Gorge

But following the conveniently presented grain of the rock, after a few thousand years the Ottauquechee was able to rasp itself through to the other side, leaving a mile-long, 165-foot-deep gorge behind. This cutting was expedited by coarse gravel in the glacial meltwater and the sheer volume of floods that carried it. Had the ridge been thicker or more resistant, Quechee Falls, by far the highest in New England, would be today's tourist attraction, not Quechee Gorge.

As for the next one-hundred-year flood, well, at this point, we don't have long to wait. And damage will be great once again given that the dams built since 1927 were designed to keep water out of the Connecticut and thus out of factories in Springfield and office buildings in Hartford, not out of art galleries and kitchenware shops in Woodstock. The miniature golf course above the gorge will still be playable though, you can count on that.

River Road along the Ottauquechee

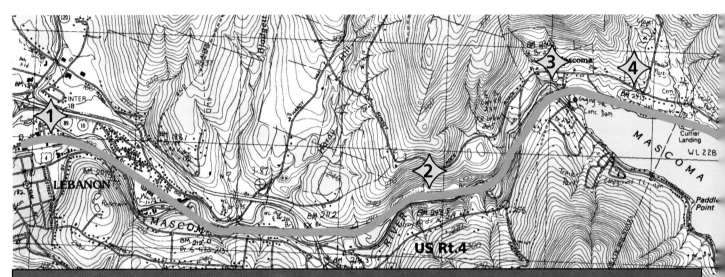

Cue the Ride . . . Northern Railtrail to Mascoma Lake

Lebanon–West Canaan and return. 15 miles, flat. Return via Crystal Lake, 20 miles. See note.

The delightful 6.5 miles of abandoned corridor from Lebanon to Enfield ranks right up with the best of the railtrail rides in the Northeast. Almost entirely removed from traveled roads, this section of the trail features seven bridge crossings, continuously rushing waters, an extensive cinder surface, and more than a mile of unspoiled frontage directly on Mascoma Lake. Brought into bikeable condition entirely by volunteers in the mid 1990s, the unheralded Northern continues to be a fascinating discovery.

East of Enfield through Canaan the trail surface alternates between cinders and stone dust, the latter laid down over unbikeable stone ballast. A deep stone cut between Canaan and Grafton marks the sixty-mile line's high point of 968 feet. A perceptible descent to Tewksbury and Kilton Ponds follows. Antique Grafton, home of an isinglass mine, is the last town in the Grafton Co. section of the trail.

Note: Looping Mascoma Lake via Crystal Lake involves a mile of Class VI "road" in Enfield. Impassable in spring, an insect Hades in summer, this section becomes reasonably passable by hybrid bike (with dismounts for exposed culverts) about Labor Day. But it's flat, as is the remaining paved mileage to Shaker Bridge.

An all-paved alternative route to Crystal Lake, via South and Ibey Roads, offers fine early architecture and a variety of views. It is not flat, however—not at all.

1. Trailhead at city rec. center/CCB. Ample parking. All services nearby.

2. Mascoma Hanging Gorge. A mini Niagara near here drained glacial Mascoma Lake, whose surface was once sixty-five feet above present river level. Now a dry falls with associated potholes, the natural feature was a Victorian-era outing favorite; may one day be open to the public again.

3. East Lebanon: "The City" until downtown Lebanon greatly developed after the RR arrived. Sawmills, slate factory, distillery, edged-tool works, bobbin mill, taverns, and boardinghouses. Note "telltales" at Payne Rd. underpass, rare survivors of early steam era. They warned roof-riding brakemen to watch their heads.

4. Ice House Rd. parking/trail access. Mascoma depot site with extensive railroad sidings, ice house, etc. All disappeared.

5. Train wreck near here, c. 1960, sent freight cars into the lake. Note initials carved in stone when rock cutting was widened, c. 1900, to accommodate bigger freight cars.

6. Baltic Mill and dam. Made woolen blankets in summer and broadcloth in winter, 1880s–1970s. Millpond geese bite the hand that feeds them.

7. Bear right at emu ranch on dirt Mud Pond Rd. (See Crystal Lake loop note.)

8. Route 4A, an old turnpike. Pres. James Monroe passed along it en route to Hanover and Montpelier, July 1817. Light traffic, one small hill.

9. Antique one-lane underpass to be removed c. 2005, with associated loss of quaintness. Return to railtrail via Bridge St.

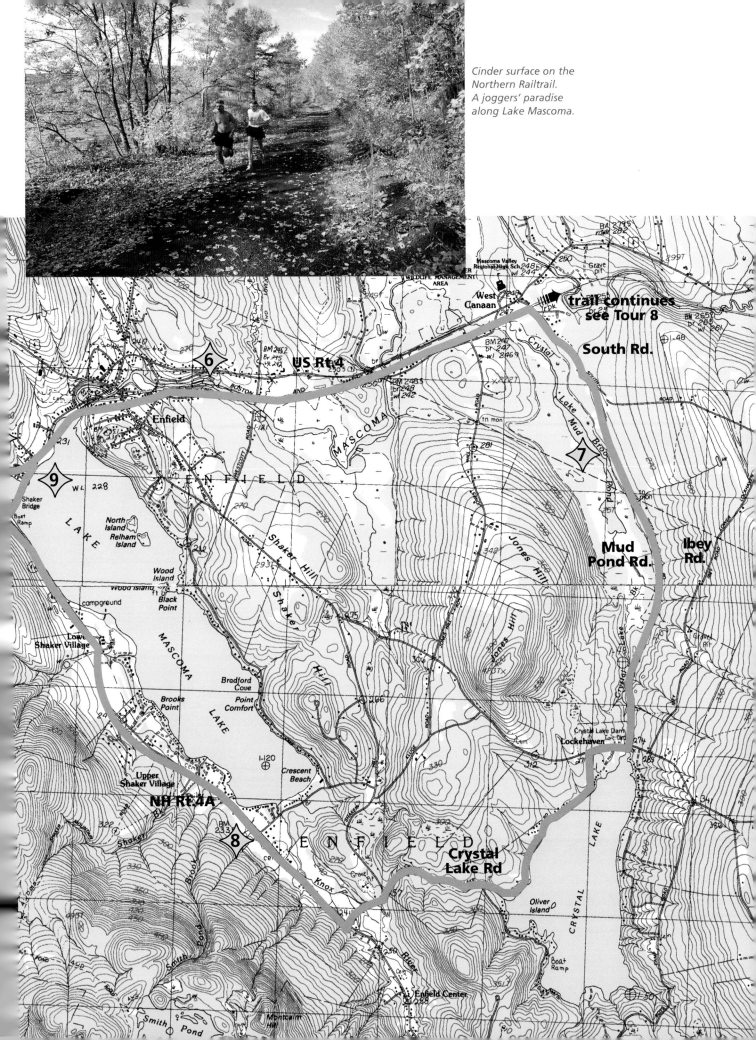

Cinder surface on the Northern Railtrail. A joggers' paradise along Lake Mascoma.

West Canaan

trail continues
see Tour 8

South Rd.

6

US Rt 4

Enfield

9

7

Mud
Pond
Rd.

Ibey
Rd.

ENFIELD

North Island
Relham Island

Wood Island

Black Point

Lower Shaker Village

MASCOMA LAKE

Bradford Cove

Point Comfort

Brooks Point

Lockehaven

Upper Shaker Village

NH Rt 4A

8

Crescent Beach

ENFIELD

Crystal Lake Rd

CRYSTAL LAKE

Oliver Island

Boat Ramp

Enfield Center

⑧ Northern Railtrail, East
Canaan-Grafton

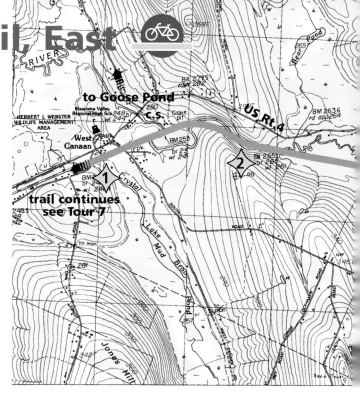

Cue the Ride . . . to Canaan

West Canaan–Grafton/Danbury. 8 miles, easiest.

Bear and moose are more likely spotted in this section of the rail corridor than to the west. In September, brilliant swamp maples around Mirror Lake frame views of glacier-burnished Mount Cardigan. **Note:** The culverts used to replace road underpasses were installed to eliminate bridge maintenance after the N.H. DOT took over the line in the 1990s. Woodchips inside the culverts ease snowmobile passage. Eastbound, the bikeable surface is being extended from Grafton to Danbury as funds become available.

1. West Canaan depot and creamery site. Parking. Two CStores nearby.

2. Excellent trailside birding along Mascoma and Indian Rivers. 1904 multiple-death wreck site ahead, with interpretation.

3. Canaan railroad yard; a major depot with water tower, coal tipple, and sidings, all now removed. An extra engine was added here to Boston-bound freight trains for the climb to the Orange height-of-land.

4. Orange cut. At 968 feet, the HOL between Concord and W.R. Jct.

5. Ruggles Mine. Mica and rare minerals dug here for centuries. Oddly interesting.

6. Trail to be extended south to Danbury in '04, and to Andover and Boscawen later. Ultimate goal: trail and rail-with-trail Concord to White River Jct., 70 miles.

Point of View

Heaven is under our feet as well as over our heads.

Thoreau, *The Pond in Winter*

Built mostly by Irish laborers who had fled the potato famine, the Northern Railroad "steam highway" reached Lebanon from Concord in 1847. Elaborate rites of celebration were held at the new downtown station at almost the exact spot where the muscle-powered bikeway begins today. Twelve hundred stockholders and guests, including the mayor of Boston, assembled to hear Daniel Webster remark on the extraordinary era that Americans then lived in: "It is altogether new. The world has seen nothing like it before."

Not in attendance at the celebration were members of a group that had inventively arranged to profit extensively from the railroad while being assured of seeing nothing of it at all—the Enfield Shakers. Despite the sect's creed of celibacy, the Enfield colony was then a vital and growing community of almost five hundred. Horrified at first when they learned the proposed railway corridor would chop their lakeside village in half, the Shaker elders later realized they were of two minds about the intrusion. Seeing great export potential for their seeds, flannel, and newly devised straight brooms, the community soon worked out an arrangement with the railroad developers to relocate the tracks on the opposite side of Mascoma Lake. Stock was purchased in the Northern Railroad Company and the deal closed with a land transfer. In thanks, the railroad named one of its brass-trimmed locos The Shaker.

The real art in the transaction came next—the building of Shaker Bridge. As the Shakers knew, the sound of the first whistle would herald Enfield's relocation from the instantly irrelevant south end of the lake to the newly modern north end. To get to the action, the Shakers built a bridge at the lake's narrow waist, the structure's design a tribute to their reputation for simplicity and innovation. First, pilings were cut and then fastened vertically around boxes of wooden cribbing. When the lake froze over, the cribs were topped off with fieldstones. Gravity then drove the piles into the muddy bottom when the whole multi-ton contraption sank at ice-out in March.

After the massive hurricane of '38 ruined the crossing's superstructure, engineers found the original pilings were in perfect condition and reused some of them in the replacement bridge. By then, the Shaker colony was gone, its doomed remnant uniting with a similarly ill-fated group in Canterbury, N.H., in 1923. Skeptics were proved right; celibacy has no future.

Orange Cut, near Tewksbury Pond, Grafton

trail continues
to Danbury

Owls Head Mountain, 1958

Cue the Ride . . . Cross Vermont Trail, West

Groton/Ricker Mills–Marshfield. 18 miles roundtrip, easy. Mountain bike.

The M&WR corridor remains almost entirely intact between the VT Rt.232–US Rt.302 intersection in Groton and Marshfield Station. The five miles of trail that begin at Ricker Pond State Park are particularly pleasant—cool woods, a pebbly surface, and views of brash, glacier-plucked Owls Head Mountain. Waterside habitat on Ricker Pond and Lake Groton hosts *Rhododendron maximum*, the only spot in N.E. where this rosy-bloomed evergreen shrub grows.

From the long-lost Lanesboro stop, the rail bed has become more of a dirt road than a trail as far as Edgewater on Marshfield Pond. Farther along, nothing remains to identify Marshfield Station either, and for good reason. At that point, the railroad grade hugs the shoulder of Knox Mt., three hundred feet above the town and the Winooski River in the valley below. There are no services along the route, although you can get down to Marshfield for a CStore soda via ass-over-teakettle Depot Street. But plan on a helluva walk back up.

Note: From Marshfield, Cross Vermont Trail loops southwest around Loveland Ledge toward Plainfield, home of ancient hippie mecca Goddard College. Some trail relocations make the course through Plainfield uncertain, but eventual connections to in-use portions in East Montpelier are assured. Between Montpelier and the Lake Champlain region, sections of the CVT are being added yearly. From Waterbury to Williston, much of the trail will follow river roads on the south side of the Winooski.

1. Ricker Mills parking area. Sawmill site, 1790 to 1963. Logs dragged to lake in winter, floated to mill in spring. State park, with camping. (The 1.5m. trail section along VT Rt.232 between Ricker Mills and US Rt.302 is also rideable. Park at CStore at intersection.)

2 Gentle climb to Lanesboro Summit begins. Some lake views.

3 Owls Head, a glacial sheepback. Ice moving from the northwest plucked stone off the face, dropping it in a boulder train to the southeast.

4. Edgewater. Through the 1940s, winter skaters and snowshoers took the train here from Montpelier for a day's outing. Trail and dirt road merge and diverge at various points.

5. Trail continues to Plainfield, Montpelier, and Burlington eventually. See note above.

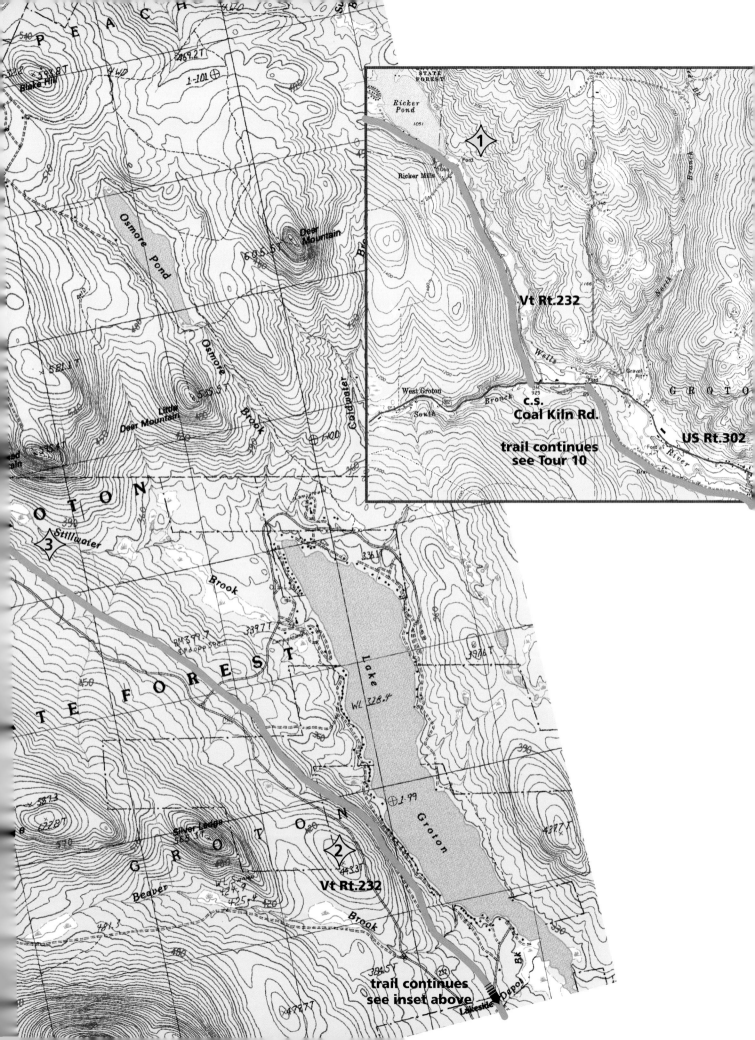

PEACH

Blake Hill

Osmore Pond

Deer Mountain

Little Deer Mountain

Osmore Brook

Coldwater Brook

STATE FOREST

Ricker Pond

Ford

Ricker Mills

Vt Rt.232

Wells

West Groton

South Branch

c.s.
Coal Kiln Rd.

Gravel Pit

GROTO

US Rt.302

River

trail continues
see Tour 10

①

Stillwater

③

Brook

FOREST

Lake

WL 328.4

Groton

Silver Ledge

GROTON

②
Vt Rt.232

Beaver

Brook

Lakeside Depot

trail continues
see inset above

RYEGATE, SCOTLAND

After a two-month voyage from the old country, two emissaries representing a group of would-be immigrants calling themselves the Scotch American Company stepped ashore at Philadelphia in May 1773. Twenty-four-year-old James Whitelaw, a surveyor, and James Allen, his assistant and numbers man, had been sent over to locate a tract where fellow lowlanders from villages along the banks of the Clyde might be able to own land. Their arrival was an everyday sort of event in America, as it had been for a century and a half. It was also not unusual that even before the men had lost their sea legs, a contact waiting on the wharf "accidentally" introduced them to one Dr. John Witherspoon. And damned if Witherspoon didn't happen to have about twenty-three thousand acres for sale "in Ryegate, in the New York Colony, upon the Connecticut River." Ownership of what was to become Vermont was then in dispute between the colonial governors of N.Y. and N.H.

A fellow Scot, who had been in America for five years, the Reverend Witherspoon was busy marketing tracts of the wilderness as part of his day job as president of nearby Princeton College. Whitelaw and Allen listened to the likeable cleric's pitch and decided to take themselves off to Ryegate on horseback, investigating various lands in Pennsylvania and upstate New York en route. By late June, they were following the Connecticut upstream, stopping at Hanover to meet Eleazar Wheelock and look over his (Indian) academy. Wheelock offered them land sufficient for thirty families gratis, saying he preferred people from old Caledonia above all others. He noted, though, that Whitelaw and Allen should make up their minds PDQ, as the country was filling up fast.

Two days later, after having walked and ridden over as much of interior Ryegate as Indian trails and blowdowns would allow, the Scotch American Company men decided the property was as good a value as they had seen. Making friends easily in nearby booming Newbury also encouraged them. Satisfied that they could stand behind their decision once back in Scotland, they soon came to terms with Witherspoon's local agent for the southern half of the township.

Ryegate was by no means uninhabited at the time, with about four hundred people having broken ground there. But most had settled along the choice river bottomlands adjoining Newbury and Bath. The coast was clear for a dozen Caledonian families to arrive the next spring, just about the time Whitelaw was completing a survey and subdivision of the company's property. Two years later, after the Scotch American Co. was a going concern, he would help build the Bayley-Hazen Military Road through Ryegate and become surveyor general of Vermont in the 1790s.

Dr. Witherspoon is said not to have made out very well in this transaction, or in any of the other land deals he was involved with on behalf of Princeton during this period. He is better remembered for a signature he executed with a group of other men at Philadelphia on July 4, 1776. Because of it, his son, John Jr., was soon called away from the six-hundred-acre tract he had taken up in the northwest corner of Ryegate just a year earlier. An aide to Washington, Witherspoon Jr. was killed at the battle of Germantown. In the meantime, Scotch American investors arriving in Boston were being detained by General Gage, who gave them the choice of returning home, passage to Nova Scotia, or enlistment in the British army.

While the Revolution only slowed the Scottish colonization of Ryegate, British conscription for the ensuing Napoleonic wars speeded it greatly. Continuing to be based in the old country, the Scotch American Company stayed in business until 1820, when all its lots had been sold. Through its efforts, hundreds of emigrants had been able to take a chance on a better life in what had by that time become Caledonia County, Vermont, U.S.A.

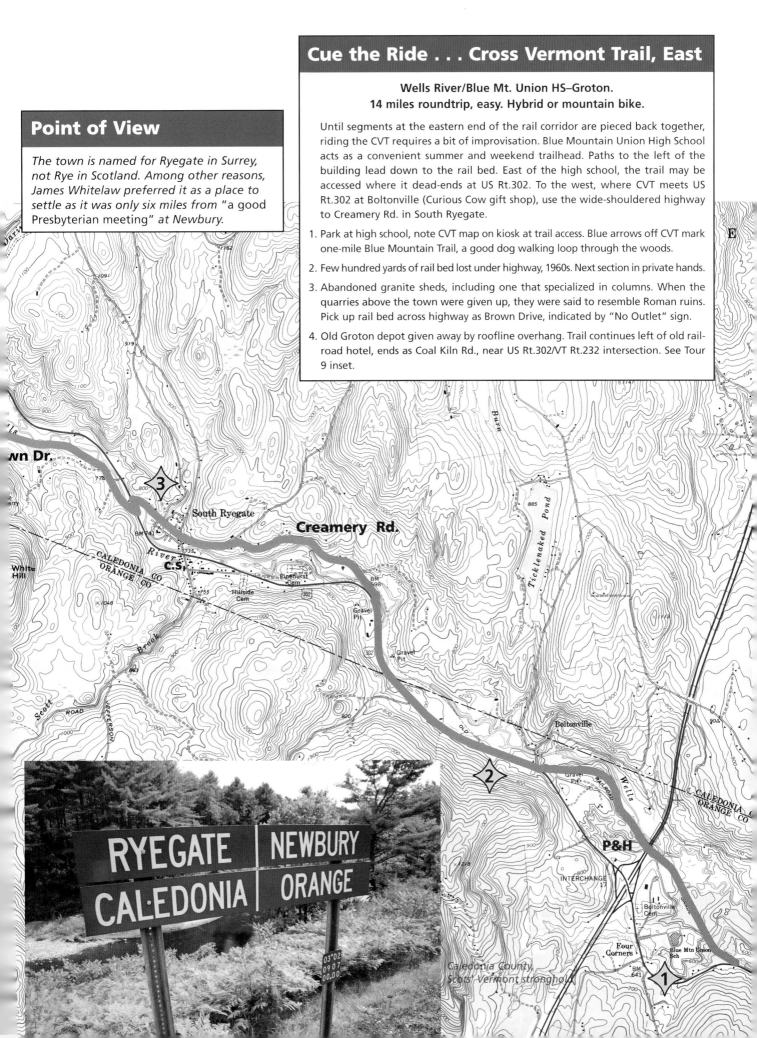

Wells River/Blue Mt. Union HS–Groton.
14 miles roundtrip, easy. Hybrid or mountain bike.

Until segments at the eastern end of the rail corridor are pieced back together, riding the CVT requires a bit of improvisation. Blue Mountain Union High School acts as a convenient summer and weekend trailhead. Paths to the left of the building lead down to the rail bed. East of the high school, the trail may be accessed where it dead-ends at US Rt.302. To the west, where CVT meets US Rt.302 at Boltonville (Curious Cow gift shop), use the wide-shouldered highway to Creamery Rd. in South Ryegate.

1. Park at high school, note CVT map on kiosk at trail access. Blue arrows off CVT mark one-mile Blue Mountain Trail, a good dog walking loop through the woods.

2. Few hundred yards of rail bed lost under highway, 1960s. Next section in private hands.

3. Abandoned granite sheds, including one that specialized in columns. When the quarries above the town were given up, they were said to resemble Roman ruins. Pick up rail bed across highway as Brown Drive, indicated by "No Outlet" sign.

4. Old Groton depot given away by roofline overhang. Trail continues left of old railroad hotel, ends as Coal Kiln Rd., near US Rt.302/VT Rt.232 intersection. See Tour 9 inset.

Point of View

The town is named for Ryegate in Surrey, not Rye in Scotland. Among other reasons, James Whitelaw preferred it as a place to settle as it was only six miles from "a good Presbyterian meeting" at Newbury.

11 Oliverian Branch Railtrail
Haverhill

COUNTRY RAILROADING BEFORE THE CIVIL WAR

Whether or not they believed their own ballyhoo, early short-line railroads like the Boston, Concord & Montreal had to appear as though they were really going someplace in order to borrow the money necessary to put pick and shovel to task out in the field. Hence, the grandiloquent BC&M moniker for a line whose wood-fired engines would never steam within sixty miles of "B" or within two hundred of "M" or near anyplace else very important. Properly, this 1840s creature should have been named the C&W—the Concord and Woodsville. But elaboration was mandatory if its promoters were to make a splash both in city financial markets and with trackside landowners in the boondocks, the latter of whom were expected to accept stock for their property, like it or not. In the scheme of things, the line was to function as a backcountry bridge route.

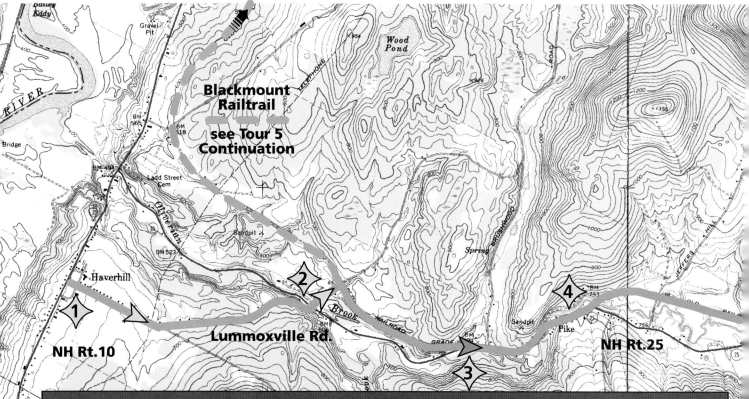

Cue the Ride . . . Oliverian Branch Railtrail

Haverhill–East Haverhill and return. 12 miles, easy. Hybrid or mountain bike.

Begin at the Haverhill Common. Ride follows NH Rt.25 from time to time. As private encroachment on nominally state-owned rail corridor varies annually, improvise a route as necessary.

1. Haverhill. Time stopped here c. 1850. Daniel Webster resided at Bliss Tavern when court was in session, practiced in what is now Alumni Hall. Ride up Court St. and bear left on Lummoxville Rd.

2. Cross NH Rt.25 and Oliverian Brook. Up the hill, go right on rail bed. (Left on rail bed leads to North Haverhill and very much mud—the Blackmount Branch, Tour 11A.)

3. Sheer drop where high stone RR bridge abutment removed for highway relocation. Dismount, follow trail down to NH Rt.25.

4. Pike. Company town 1840s–1920s. Made whetstones from mica schist quarried on hill to the south, shipped worldwide. Smokestack built 1899, a time when the Pike Co. dictated all houses were to be yellow and white for sunshine and purity. Rail bed begins below highway opposite circled "25" on map.

5. Pick up rail line at camping area. Birch-lined causeway through wetlands paved with mayflowers in spring. Viewing areas for warblers, blue heron, wood ducks, snipe, and moose.

6. Trail ends near dam. Picnic tables, porta-san. Return via railtrail or highway.

It would connect the new Concord RR, which ran from that city to Boston, and the Connecticut & Passumpsic RR, which had recently snaked its way upriver from the newly devised town of White River Jct. to Wells River. When and if the C&P's designs on extending farther north through Vermont to Canada were realized, the BC&M would be billed as the shortest route to Quebec from Boston.

Like other startup N.H. railroad combines, the BC&M directors had to overcome another problem besides financing before the dirt turning could begin. The retrograde N.H. legislature wasn't overly enthusiastic about chartering railroads. After all, it was a newfangled contraption *and bein' as how railroads would compete with the stagecoaches 'n' all, dontcha know,* lengthy cogitation was perhaps warranted. Finally, after spending years fruitlessly trying to get up a head of steam under the statehouse dome, five different lines anxious to begin issuing stock brought in (by stagecoach) Dartmouth Professor C.B. "Fishbreath" Haddock to talk sense to the provincial minds there. After acquainting elected officials with the news that travel by rail would be more convenient and lead to a major increase in land values, candles went on in enough eighteenth-century top-hatted heads so that all five lines were chartered forthwith.

Building north towards Woodsville, beginning in 1848, the BC&M's road soon reached Meredith on Lake Winnipesaukee, but two years went by before the work engine arrived at Plymouth. The line limped into Warren a year later, construction abruptly ceasing in the pucker brush there as the funding well ran dry. Postponing the laying of more Welsh-manufactured rail, the directors headed for the financial printers for fresh coin of the realm—sheaves of floridly decorated railroad bonds. More paper had to be peddled to fund a $150,000 rock cut at Warren's Ore Hill. On the other side lay Oliverian Brook and the long descent through Haverhill to a meeting with the C&P on the Connecticut. Finally, the slow and expensive wagon and drover route over the paralleling Coos Turnpike would be superseded, with a short-line route to Canada from Boston in the offing.

By this time, though, the rail line up ahead, along the Vermont side of the Connecticut, had other ideas. In significant debt to the Northern RR (Tours 7 & 8), which operated from Concord to White River Jct., the C&P had no intention of allowing a Northern competitor to cross over from N.H. and force an interchange with its tracks at Wells River.

In the summer of 1852, its paper successfully peddled and Ore Hill blasted through with black powder, the upstart BC&M began erecting a bridge on the Connecticut two miles south of Woodsville. It planned to come ashore on the Vermont side, just upstream from where the noted Leete family round-barn farm is today. But lying in wait on the opposite shore was the C&P's president, who also happened to be Vermont's governor. Once the presumptuous BC&M had expended time and money on a wooden trestle, he dispatched a gang of roughnecks to fell trees and mound up a hill of dirt in the right-of-way. A superior force of BC&M Irish demolished the barricade—twice—before a deal was struck. The interloping line would build a bridge at Woodsville proper (that very curious rail-on-top, horse-drawn-traffic-below affair noted earlier) and the two lines would then merge, splitting freight bound for Concord.

Over the next forty years, the Boston, Concord & Montreal enjoyed but a few days in the sun before its inevitable merger with northern New England's big tooter, the Boston & Maine RR. The BC&M's imported rails were light and had soft spots throughout, and its green ties rotted away after only a few seasons. Soon the nearby hillsides were bare, clear-cut for cordwood for high-wheeled engines evocatively named Moosilauk, Lady of the Lake, and Winnepisogee. The Coos Turnpike had been outflanked, to be sure, and the cost of shipping the valley's bounty cut by two-thirds. Indeed, nearly everyone benefited from the building of the railroad except the stage companies and, of course, the stockholders. When last heard of, they were being asked by the directors to accept a new kind of paper, something called a "sinking fund debenture." Abandoned in 1954, the BC&M's traffic was rerouted to the Northern line, which was itself to survive for only twenty more years.

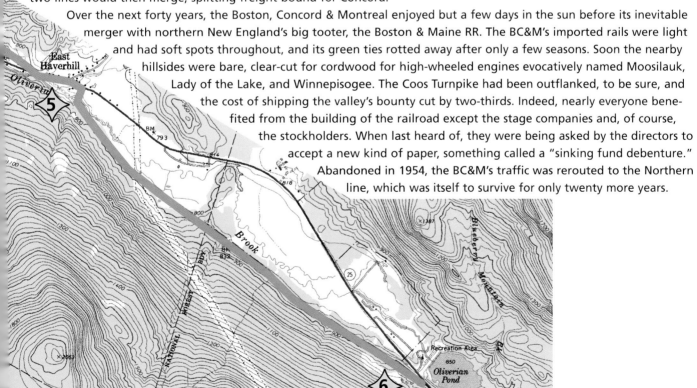

Within a half-century of the settlement of northwestern New England, what had been thought of as little but foreboding woods began to attract travelers who took note of the region's natural and manmade beauty. Although crude dwellings, pig-trodden dooryards, and stony fields lined with root-festooned stumps were still the rule, refinements were in the offing. Income from the sheep explosion and growing food exports to industrializing southern New England began to show up in fine domestic and public architecture, painted fences, and groomed pastures.

At first the wealth arrived via the flatboats that carried southbound trade to New Haven and from there to England and the Caribbean. After 1800, country produce also flowed down from the Vermont hill farms, across the river on ferries and covered bridges to the N.H. turnpikes, and on toward Portsmouth and Boston. Although this era lasted only a generation, the idealization of rural New England—and Vermont in particular—as a Peaceable Kingdom inhabited by yeoman farmers and village gentlefolk endures to this day.

But the reality of the next hundred years was quite different. As one observer noted, "If North America had been settled from west to east, New England would never have been farmed." Before 1820, subsistence farming took many hands, but the sheep-raising era that followed only required the clearing of more land, no matter how steep it might be. When the farmers' sons were finished felling the last of the virgin woods, they had no more to do. Nor was there any wage labor to be found upcountry, since there were no factories to speak of yet. So the boys pulled a Horace Greeley, hitting the road for the flat land and deep soil of Ohio. Their sisters left soon after, walking behind cartloads of their families' wool to the mills of Lowell and Lawrence. In 1850, 40 percent of native-born Vermonters lived elsewhere. The Great Swarming had given way to the Great U-Turn.

By the time of the Civil War, railroads made it far cheaper to ship farm products to the new cities, but in some ways, things were even worse. Cheap freight meant competing with one's relatives in Lebanon, Iowa, and in Vermont, Illinois was impossible. And now, due to inheritance, many farms were smaller and even less profitable. Large-scale dairying blossomed, particularly after ice-cake lockers were built into freight cars, but rural life continued to be Hardscrabble and Poor Farm, as the names of the back roads we rediscover today testify. Bucolic imagery intensified nonetheless, thanks to early photographers' search for rustic imagery. As town and national anniversaries arrived, nostalgia took hold. Centennial Farm designations and Old Home Days celebrated a past that rarely had been as sunny as the posters glued to covered bridge walls made it seem.

By 1890, fifteen hundred farms in New Hampshire were abandoned or vacant. In one twenty-year period, the number of Vermont farms was halved, a sensible option in hindsight since it was the poorest land that was being forsaken. So much of the Green Mountain State was unproductive that the legislature advertised it in Europe at $3–$5 an acre. A hundred years before, prime land in the Champlain Valley had sold for three times that. Even so, there were few takers, as "dirt-cheap" became an ironic bull's-eye. Stone-rich New England was weak competition for the western railroads and their boundless trans-Mississippi holdings.

At the time of WWI, tinted prints of overflowing August hayricks and steam rising out of sugar shacks in March, churned out by mythologizer Wallace Nutting, spoke of prosperity, but it was only an illusion. Forty years of damn poor sledding were ahead. Until the interstates unspooled themselves north, no matter how cheery Norman Rockwell may have sketched it for his art director clients in Madison Avenue publishing houses, rural N.H. and almost all of Vermont couldn't be painted as anything but dirt poor. As geologists were then discovering, the Greens and Whites proved to be just an extension of the flinty Appalachia.

And with that, it was also noticed that something else had happened. Where husbandry had flourished and then withered, a wooded landscape had grown up, obscuring and disguising the past. Later—a generation later—new pilgrims would find their way to the lost foundations of this New England that once was. They would poke through wracked barns, picnic at millraces gone dry, and push bicycles along farm lanes overgrown with briars. Invigorated by their discoveries, these explorers would sidle through the underbrush of the decades and unearth a rosy past that never was and pronounce it Eden all over again.

East Corinth, July

Cue the Ride . . . East of Eden

East Corinth–East Topsham and return.
16 miles, easy. Any bike. From Bradford, 31m.

Once novices get the biking bug on railtrails and bike-ways, the open road is not far behind. A perfect starter trip, this eight-mile pedal along the Tabor branch of the Waits River offers everything cyclists new to the road could want—fine scenery, good pavement, no traffic, and a few small hills to crow about afterward. The prevailing wind even blows in the right direction. More serious enthusiasts will set out from I-91 Exit 16 in Bradford, along VT Rt.25, adding fifteen miles to the outing. Everyone should bring a picnic.

1. *Beetle Juice* exteriors shot on hilltop, 1986, with village as backdrop.

2. Cows cross road here, now and again, to be milked. A rare sight these days.

3. To Bradford, 13.5m., via Swamp, Fuller, and North Rds., paved/dirt. Exceptional views. See Tour 39.

4. Devils Den. Cave with a good story to it. Ask an old-timer.

5. East Topsham. Eat picnic on bench at old blacksmith shop. Listen to brook, smell horses, watch phoebe pair flicking tails on telephone wire. Wait for car to come by. Enjoy shade, go home, tell no one.

Point of View

Cycle tracks will abound in Utopia.

H.G. Wells

to Bradford
13.5 mi

Vt Rt.25

Vt Motif #2
Waits River

East Corinth

Vt Rt.25
Bradford, 7.5 mi

Waits River Vermont Motif #2
second most photographed scene in Vermont

⑬ Cornish Colony
St. Gaudens & Aspet

Elegantly named by his Irish mother and French shoemaker father for the great artist he was to become, Augustus St. Gaudens arrived in New York in 1848, age six months. At only thirteen years, the gifted boy was apprenticed to a local cameo cutter, beginning his studies to become a sculptor at l'Ecole Nationale Supérieure des Beaux-Arts in Paris six years later. His professional career was launched when he gained his first commissions in Rome soon after. At age thirty-three, his first major work, a monument to Admiral Farragut in New York, was hailed as a stylistic breakthrough, bringing him almost instant success.

In the spring of 1885, St. Gaudens was enticed to Cornish for a look-see by New York lawyer and friend Charles Beaman. Beaman was promoting the area as a summer colony, renting out various cheaply-owned, played-out farms to the kind of creative people he liked. The sculptor and his wife were driven over from the Windsor station to view Huggins' Folly, a decrepit brick pile that had been put up on speculation eighty years before. At the time, the Huggins brothers anticipated a turnpike would pass their door en route from the nearby Cornish-Windsor Bridge to Newport. The turnpike never materialized, and by 1830, the Hugginses had departed for Illinois. Turned off by the forbidding appearance of the main house—it was mud season—

Cue the Ride . . . Cornish Colony

Plainfield–Cornish Loop.
20 miles, moderate. Road bike. Ride clockwise.

Quiet all-paved country road loops are hard to find. But except for a couple of miles on NH Rts.120 and 12-A, this ride is the exception. Even more unusual, when riding clockwise, an elevation gain of four hundred feet is spread out over almost ten miles—hardly noticeable. The side trip to the St. Gaudens site angles straight up, but the exertion to get there will soon be forgotten. Oh yes, there's a rather significant covered bridge along this route too.

Note: Deserted Old River Rd., paralleling NH Rt.12-A to the west, comes highly recommended for pleasant Sunday afternoon rides and brisk walks. But do not loop back to Plainfield via 12-A from the north end of it, except on mid-summer Sunday mornings well before 7:00—no shoulder, big hills, fast traffic.

1. Plainfield lost half its population between 1860 and 1920. *A Walking Tour of Plainfield,* a brochure available at the village store, includes a fine map and architectural narrative. Daniels Rd. offers a shortcut to Stage Rd.

2. Columbus Jordan Rd., mountain bike route on Class VI road to noted views at French's Ledges. Turn right ahead at town garage onto Penniman Rd.

3. Cornish Flat, classic nineteenth-century crossroads village, with sawmills, grist mills, tanneries, creameries, carriage building, harness making, etc.

4. No shoulder along one mile of NH Rt.120. Right turn on Center Rd., easy to miss.

5. St. Gaudens site, half-mile uphill.

6. Scenic Platt Rd. through estate area becomes Thrasher Rd. in Plainfield. Two walking hills.

7. Squag City bypass to Salinger's place. Directions: Right at covered bridge underpass, then second left at wholistic manure farm, Snipe Hunt Rd. Can't miss it—only house done up in camo.

St. Gaudens did see possibilities in the barn as a studio. At the insistence of his wife, he took the property for the summer for $500. By August, Augustus considered the move a great stroke of luck, but was unable to convince Beaman to sell the property until ten years later. His landlord and patron finally accepted $2,500, asking also for a portrait of himself to be done in bas-relief, the sculptural form for which St. Gaudens had by then become preeminent in the world.

By that time also, the artist's reputation had identified the slopes overlooking the Connecticut River and Mt. Ascutney as a premier artists colony, conveniently located only five hours from Grand Central Station. Painters and sculptors were the first to show up in Cornish and nearby Plainfield. Writers arrived in the 1890s, followed shortly after by plain old rich people in the decade before World War I. Throughout the boom, property values shot up, social calendars were full all season, and everybody got work, particularly local tradesmen. The latter were recruited at $1 a day or less to erect the New York–architect-designed mansions that dot the hillsides of the two towns today. Other than its founder, the best-known name associated with the Cornish colony's history is Maxfield Parrish, the illustrator son of painter Stephen Parrish, who had arrived in 1893. (Not to forget the last of this line of artsy celebrities, a certain writer with the initials J.D.S. See Cue 7.)

While this gathering of talent was going on, St. Gaudens was transforming Huggins' Folly into Aspet, a showy mansion. Annual additions and modifications stunned the Cornish hayseeds. They continued to refer to its purported one-time use as a whorehouse, out of city folks' hearing, of course. Pillars, piazzas, and pergolas went up, and gardens and hedges sprouted. A golf course, bowling green, and toboggan run were installed, as well as a proper studio that could accommodate the artist's many assistants, replacing the barn in 1904. By then, St. Gaudens had been diagnosed with cancer and was in residence at Aspet year-round. Among the masterpieces created in the last twenty years of his life, St. Gaudens's Shaw Memorial, installed along Boston Common in 1900, remains his best-known work.

Today the main house, still shaded by a honey locust planted in 1886 (now N.H. State Champion), retains much of its original furnishings and decorative objects. Overall, as interpreted by the National Park Service, the Arcadian St. Gaudens site stands as the premier artistic destination in the region and testimony to the truism that the whole is more than the sum of its parts.

Note: *During the Sunday afternoon concert series on the lawn during the summer, the studios remain open but the main house is closed.*

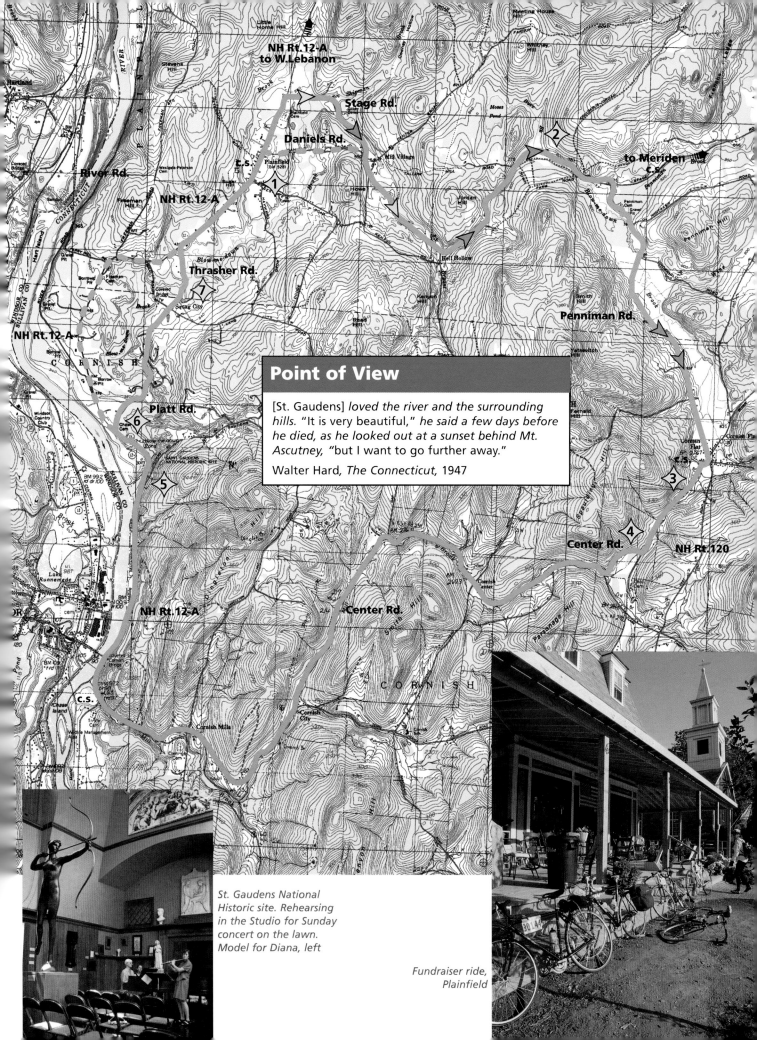

NH Rt.12-A
to W.Lebanon

Stage Rd.

Daniels Rd.

2

to Meriden
c.s.

River Rd.

NH Rt.12-A

1

Thrasher Rd.

7

Penniman Rd.

NH Rt. 12-A

Platt Rd.

6

5

3

4

Center Rd.

NH Rt.120

NH Rt. 12-A

Center Rd.

c.s.

Point of View

[St. Gaudens] *loved the river and the surrounding hills. "It is very beautiful,"* he said a few days before he died, as he looked out at a sunset behind Mt. Ascutney, *"but I want to go further away."*

Walter Hard, *The Connecticut,* 1947

St. Gaudens National Historic site. Rehearsing in the Studio for Sunday concert on the lawn. Model for Diana, left

Fundraiser ride, Plainfield

As if President Franklin Roosevelt didn't have enough problems in 1939—imminent war in Europe, a resurgent Depression, and a Supreme Court that was overturning his New Deal initiatives—along comes Union Village. Now, Union Village wasn't any more of a town yesterday than it is today—just barely a hamlet, in fact. And nothing of consequence was happening, nor had ever happened, there in the one hundred fifty years of its extremely modest existence. Boondocks, you say? As late as 1917, the way to get to Hanover was by horse-drawn stage. But, once again, geography was destiny and U.V. hit the front pages coast to coast. How so?

Well, after monster floods in 1927 and 1936 sluiced out much of the Connecticut River drainage, the Army Corps of Engineers proposed a series of flood control dams on tributaries like the Ompompanoosuc. This made good sense to everybody locally and downcountry. Yes, the dam would primarily protect Massachusetts and Connecticut cities far downstream, but that was OK with Vermont. What put two Thetford selectmen who lived in Union Village on the warpath was the possibility the government might—just might—want to generate power at this here dam too. As with almost all federally financed dams, penstocks (pipes that carry water to generators) had been included in the design, but no powerhouse was planned. Penstocks are standard operating procedure, said the Corps, and we really must insist.

No you don't! screamed an apoplectic Governor George Aiken, for reasons that are still not clear but had mostly to do with turf, apparently. Volleys of "Don't Tread on Me" began to be fired toward the nation's capital from Montpelier. Citing the Green Mountain Boys' devotion to liberty and principle of states' rights (the latter to the enormous satisfaction of the Jim Crow South), the Vermont legislature approved a defense fund and petitioned Congress to preclude federal power development permanently.

In no time, Union Village, in some ways more fictional than Grovers Corners, became national front-page news. Governor Aiken quickly assumed the role of Joan of Arc and seemed to relish it. Pundits began to mention him as a Republican candidate for president in 1940. The maple leaf would be his symbol, akin to the Democrats' use of the sunflower in 1936. From below the Mason-Dixon line, the Sons of Confederate Veterans declared they had "waited long for so valiant a champion to appear on the national stage."

At that point, with the feds cast as the bully, FDR backed off, suggesting that if Vermont had second thoughts, the dam money could go to any number of other states that needed it. A Vermont state senator then offered the best perspective on what had become a theater-of-the-absurd dustup. He proposed appropriating the money to equip "two-fisted he-men and she-women with blunderbusses for the defense of the sacred bog, swamp or morass known as the Village of Union."

With Roosevelt stepping back from a fight that did little but re-energize Republican images of him as a would-be dictator, the tempest over sacred reed beds on the Thetford side of the Norwich border moved to the inside pages. In any case, war soon interrupted New England flood control planning, and a powerless Union Village Dam finally was completed a decade later. The hamlet retreated back into obscurity, and today the affair is entirely forgotten.

Oddly, at just the same time government power was being precluded at Union Village, private utilities, long vilified by all levels of government as the evils of monopoly incarnate, were extensively enlarging Wilder Dam a few miles downstream on the Connecticut solely for electricity generation.

The Wilder approval process had bred years of controversy of its own. This time, instead of two selectmen from Union Village bending the governor's ear, the special pleaders were a committee of agrarians bemoaning the loss of bottomlands to be covered by a new forty-six-mile Wilder Lake. Their arguments for

Cue the Ride . . . Damn Village

Union Village Dam Recreation Area
Pompanoosuc–Thetford Center and return.
11 miles, moderate difficulty. From Ledyard Bridge, 21 miles.

Hill-wise, dirt Campbell Flat Rd. has a few short, steep pitches, but all are well shaded. Myriad trails within the U.V. dam reservation are worth following; one leads to the bones of an old farm bought out by the Engineers.

Note: The suggested loop that includes Thetford Center to Thetford Hill requires a 400-foot climb for about a mile. More than a walking hill, this is serious business. Catch a ride in a pickup truck instead. If you notice any self-contained long-distance bike tourers tackling Thetford Hill, they are following Adventure Cycling's cross-country route. Cheer them on—only 275 more miles to Bar Harbor.

Also, as suggested by the map, Tucker Hill Rd. leads to the north entrance of the dam property and damn good swimming.

1. Park along VT Rt.132, explore railroad loop. "Kendall," the old station name, was chosen because it fit on a timetable better than Ompompanoosuc. Kendall was the stationmaster.

2. Walking hill to gated dam-site entry. Dirt road to Thetford Center.

3. One of several swimming holes, this one a popular nudie spot in hippie daze.

4. "Union" refers to early school straddling the town lines of Norwich and Thetford.

5. Not as flat as it looks on the map.

preservation wouldn't hold water, however, since tens of thousands of acres nearby in both states had lain fallow for decades. To show sympathy to rural interests, a congressional committee took testimony from Connecticut River Valley farmers in 1949, but up along the Connecticut, concrete was already being poured.

Academy Hill Rd., Union Village. Avid cyclists of the Hanover Morning Group, climbing toward Thetford Hill.

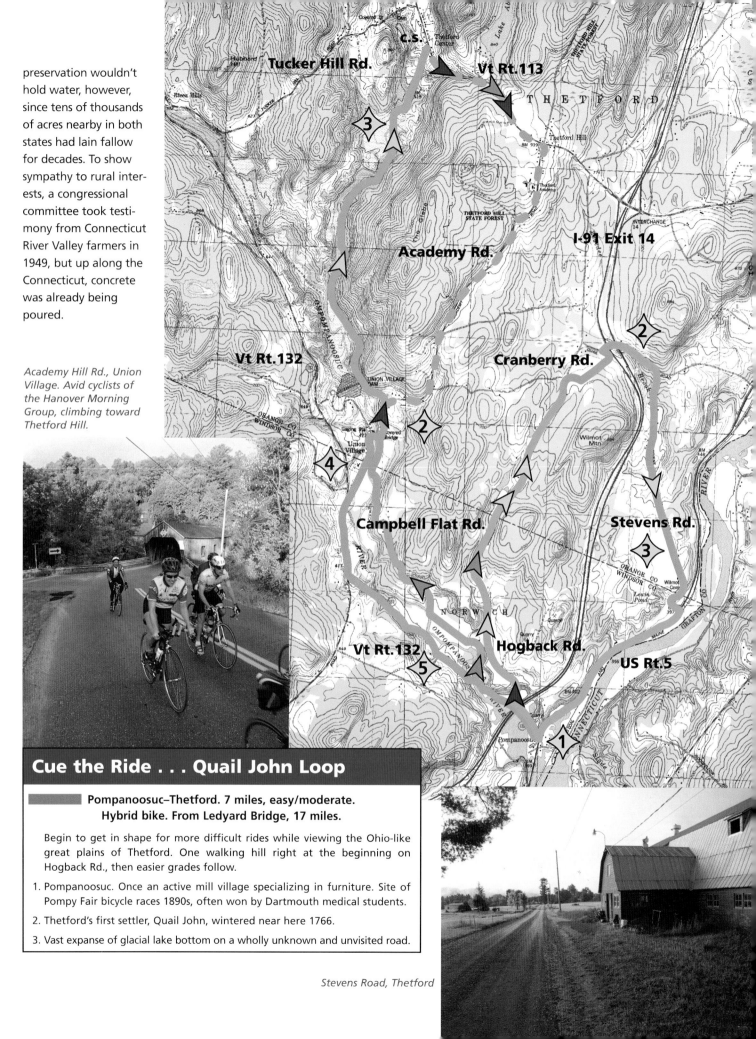

Tucker Hill Rd.

Vt Rt.113

Academy Rd.

I-91 Exit 14

Vt Rt.132

Cranberry Rd.

Campbell Flat Rd.

Stevens Rd.

Vt Rt.132

Hogback Rd.

US Rt.5

Cue the Ride . . . Quail John Loop

Pompanoosuc–Thetford. 7 miles, easy/moderate. Hybrid bike. From Ledyard Bridge, 17 miles.

Begin to get in shape for more difficult rides while viewing the Ohio-like great plains of Thetford. One walking hill right at the beginning on Hogback Rd., then easier grades follow.

1. Pompanoosuc. Once an active mill village specializing in furniture. Site of Pompy Fair bicycle races 1890s, often won by Dartmouth medical students.

2. Thetford's first settler, Quail John, wintered near here 1766.

3. Vast expanse of glacial lake bottom on a wholly unknown and unvisited road.

Stevens Road, Thetford

(16) Embarrassment of Riches: The Dirt Roads of Norwich

Norwich's remarkable set of dirt bicycling roads rises out from the village center like a pianist's right hand splayed wide. Bragg Hill Road juts hard left as the thumb; index finger Turnpike Road points north to the aerie on Gile Mountain; middle finger Upper Turnpike reaches for the Strafford border; and ring finger New Boston has an old broken knuckle at the turn for Norford Lake. As the odd digit, little finger Bradley Hill Road zooms up for mountain views from its stubbed-off base near the old village center on the Union Village Road.

As a group, these old tracks help us imagine how the glacier was rebuffed by the hard rocks of 1,800-foot Griggs Mountain on the western border of Norwich. Taking the path of least resistance, the flowing ice concentrated its power on routing out a suite of parallel valleys in softer, lower rocks to the east. (Never underestimate a glacier. Pebbles of Barre granite can be found in Bragg Brook; that's a carry from the nearest source of at least 25 miles.) As with the anatomy of the entire region, east-west connections between the fingers aren't numerous but are sufficient for innumerable variations on the theme of up and back from Dan & Whit's General Store.

April goop, Gile Mountain, Norwich

Point of View

*Get a bicycle.
You certainly will not
regret it, if you live.*

Mark Twain

June evening, Jericho Road

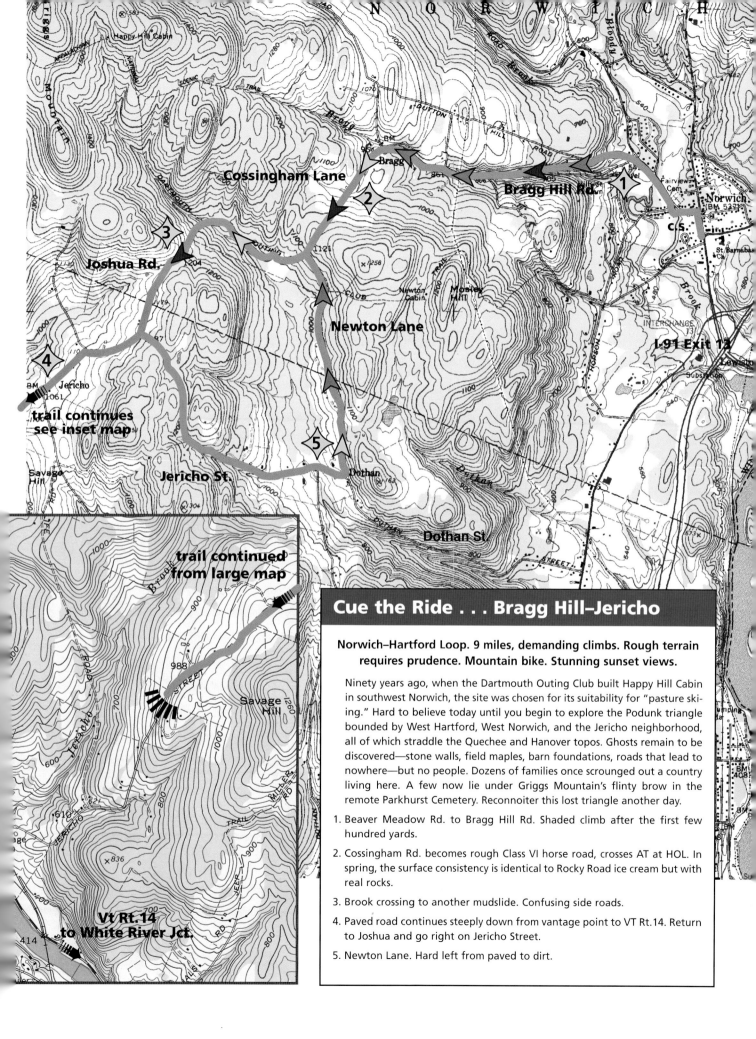

Cue the Ride . . . Bragg Hill–Jericho

Norwich–Hartford Loop. 9 miles, demanding climbs. Rough terrain requires prudence. Mountain bike. Stunning sunset views.

Ninety years ago, when the Dartmouth Outing Club built Happy Hill Cabin in southwest Norwich, the site was chosen for its suitability for "pasture skiing." Hard to believe today until you begin to explore the Podunk triangle bounded by West Hartford, West Norwich, and the Jericho neighborhood, all of which straddle the Quechee and Hanover topos. Ghosts remain to be discovered—stone walls, field maples, barn foundations, roads that lead to nowhere—but no people. Dozens of families once scrounged out a country living here. A few now lie under Griggs Mountain's flinty brow in the remote Parkhurst Cemetery. Reconnoiter this lost triangle another day.

1. Beaver Meadow Rd. to Bragg Hill Rd. Shaded climb after the first few hundred yards.

2. Cossingham Rd. becomes rough Class VI horse road, crosses AT at HOL. In spring, the surface consistency is identical to Rocky Road ice cream but with real rocks.

3. Brook crossing to another mudslide. Confusing side roads.

4. Paved road continues steeply down from vantage point to VT Rt.14. Return to Joshua and go right on Jericho Street.

5. Newton Lane. Hard left from paved to dirt.

Norwich: 3 Rides

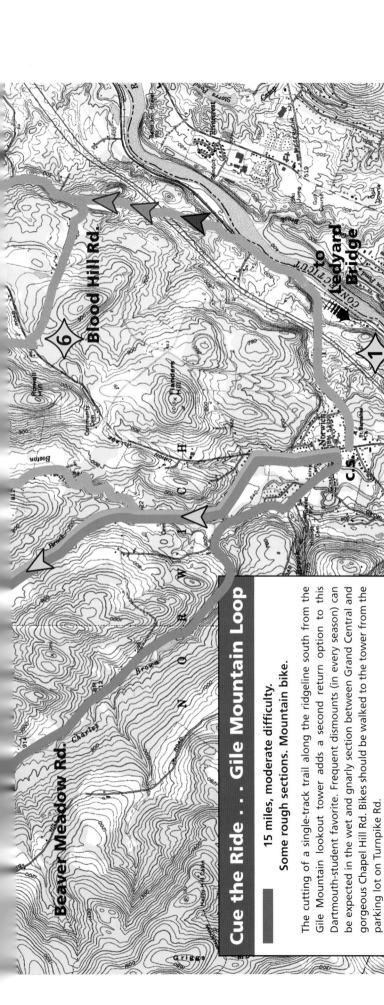

Beaver Meadow Rd.

Blood Hill Rd.

to Ledyard Bridge

CONNECTICUT

I-91 Exit 13

Cue the Ride . . . Gile Mountain Loop

**15 miles, moderate difficulty.
Some rough sections. Mountain bike.**

The cutting of a single-track trail along the ridgeline south from the Gile Mountain lookout tower adds a second return option to this Dartmouth-student favorite. Frequent dismounts (in every season) can be expected in the wet and gnarly section between Grand Central and gorgeous Chapel Hill Rd. Bikes should be walked to the tower from the parking lot on Turnpike Rd.

1. Jones Tavern, 1802. Hard dirt begins.
2. Parking. Fire tower repaired 2002. Panoramic views.
3. Alternate single-track trail to Beaver Meadow Rd.; route uncertain.
4. Large puddles. Rough, rocky descent.
5. White-robed Rolling Pilgrim sect met here on Sunday mornings 1830s. See regionalist artist Paul Sample's *Beaver Meadow* (1939) at Dartmouth's Hood Museum.

Cue the Ride . . . Pattrell Road–Bradley Hill Road Loop

14 miles, tough climbs. Some rough sections. Mountain or hybrid bike.

1. From Ledyard Bridge.
2. Slafter House, 1786; originally hip-roofed. See *Early Houses of Norwich*, p. 33.
3. CAUTION! T-intersection on steep downhill. Union Village/VT Rt.132 1.5m to the right.
4. Site of "trail or road" squabble between town and developer, 2000–201_?
5. Class VI. Ledge on downhill. Dismount. Views from peak of Bradley Hill, then precipitous descent to another T-intersection at Union Village Rd. Jog left to Blood Hill Rd.
6. Partially abandoned. Mud, hidden potholes. Cooper's hawks commonly seen here. Sheep ahead.

Cue the Ride . . . Upper Turnpike–Norford Lake Loop

17 miles, moderate difficulty. Mountain bike.

No views, but no cars or people either. Shaded. A scenic motoring loop can be made by using New Boston Rd. instead of Upper Turnpike.

1. Jones Rd. to Upper Turnpike.
2. Woods trail after last house. Slippery ledge on the downhill. Dismount.
3. Fine headstones, sylvan setting.
4. Return via paved New Boston Rd. Dirt Ladeau Rd. connects to Tour 18.

News of a "copperas" find in Orange County, Vermont reached speculators in Boston soon after 1800. Local farm folk gathering maple sap on an unnamed hill had come upon orange snow in the woods near the four-corner border of Strafford, Norwich, Thetford, and Sharon. Returning later in the spring with pick and shovel, they exposed a deposit of copper sulfate, the mineral then known as copperas. Excellent for tanning buffalo hides, freshening up out-houses, and worming both man and beast, when pre-pared in liquid form it was sold generically as "green vitriol," essentially a kind of sulfuric acid.

To exploit what was hoped to be a sizeable deposit, Harvard Medical School graduate Amos Binney of Boston put together an investor group to buy the site. He then hired chemical manufacturer and copperas patent-holder Isaac Tyson of Baltimore to set up a mill

Cue the Ride . . . Elizabeth Mine

South Strafford–Elizabeth Mine–Turnpike Rd. Loop.
7 miles or so, paved; dirt, rocks, mud, standing water in spring.
Mountain bike. Moderate to difficult. Ride clockwise.

Like Tour 21 that follows, this journey is designed to be as much an explo-ration of abandoned New England as it is a bicycle ride. Expect to get off your bike and walk, not only for road conditions and steepness but in order to go toe-to-toe with the past.

1. Strafford finally electrified in 1930. Lines followed Mine Rd. to Tyson family mansion Buena Vista, and then on to their mine. Do the same.

2. First building on right in mine complex was infirmary. Bear right on Copperas Road through diggings. Acid-resistant white birch and its kin first colonizers of the wasteland ahead.

3. Grand Central, a mud hole of abandoned roads on the Strafford/Norwich border. See Tour 17.

4. Bouldery transitional walking section down to town-maintained Turnpike Rd.

and kilns on what was then the "New" Boston Road. Tyson, a relentless experimenter, hoped to improve upon the method for smelting out copper as a pure metal. He also planned to make money for his backers by producing venetian red, a scarce paint pig-ment. Vitriol, which was to be the mine's leading product, had a ready market as a purgative; one purveyor sold it as Professor Hulme's Bowel Auger. To accomplish his goals, Tyson imported equipment and supplies, including anthracite coal, via flatboat up the Connecticut River, which was then outfitted with locks as far north as Wilder.

At first, ore was dug right from the surface on the side of a hill. Later, a shaft was sunk and new extraction methods attempted, but no great fortunes were made in Strafford. The pursuit continued nonetheless along what was by then known nationally as "Copperas Brook," running below "Copperas Hill" and on down to "Copper Flat" on the west branch of the Pompy. Money poured in, but a financial crash during the Van Buren presidency in the 1830s ended Tyson's attempt at innovation. The mine sputtered along thereafter as various prospectors repeatedly missed the mother lode.

In the 1870s, the Copperfield mine in Vershire, seven miles to the north, rose to great prominence. With that, a second-generation Tyson returned to have a go at it, finding enough success to build Buena Vista, a mansion on Mine Road that still stands. Electrification brought renewed interest in Vermont copper around 1900, with George Westinghouse investing a million dollars in fur-nace technology up the road at Vershire. Others did the same in Strafford on a smaller scale at what became known as the Elizabeth Mine, renamed after a Tyson.

The heyday of copper mining at the Elizabeth began in 1943 when government geologists reprised the original discovery by dragging drilling equipment up the hill on a sap-gathering sled. Pay dirt was struck a thousand feet down, and, after new opera-tors invested heavily in effective extraction technol-ogy, the mine became a huge producer of concentrated ore until abandoned in 1958.

In the 1990s, brooks running orange with acid pol-lution finally got the Environmental Protection Agency's attention. Differences arose over plans to cap the vast tailing pile at what was now deemed a Superfund site. But, as with almost all public affairs in Vermont, closure would not come easily or soon.

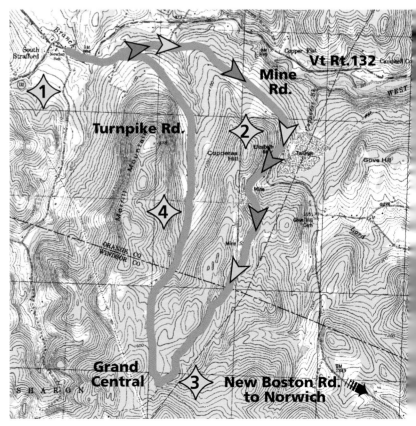

Bald as a grape a century ago, the Thetford hill country along the Strafford border has been gone-to-seed and abandoned roads for decades. Begin this exploration of it almost anywhere: at Thetford Center to warm up via roller-coaster Tucker Hill Rd., or at the Union Village Dam north entry for a swim afterward, or from South Strafford four miles west on VT Rt.132. A clockwise loop is suggested as it avoids climbing super-steep Pero Road.

Philosophically, after leaving VT Rt.132 at Jackson Brook Rd., a short, perky climb leads to an abandoned woods track of the best type—a series of stepped rises, old walls, and good drainage.

Cue the Ride . . . Thetford Woods

Thetford Center–Rices Mills Loop. 9.5 miles, moderate. Two major climbs (see narrative), some rough going. Mountain bike.

1. Union Village Dam north entry. River access, parking. Walking and biking trails, swimming holes.

2. Jackson Brook Rd. Becomes a woods road at .4 miles; conditions may vary.

3. Downhill, with ledge, moss-covered rocks, and washouts, requires dismount. Steep descent on Pero Rd. past junkyard (mostly Ford) to T-intersection. Right on Sawnee Bean Rd. a third of a mile to Poor Farm Rd.

4. Poor Farm no longer contiguous to Tucker Hill Rd., becomes Whipporwill Rd. instead. Moderate grades, selection of junkyards-to-be, including MoPar.

Opportunistic poplar is absent here, crowded out by hardwoods, though some pine, good for nothing but chipping, darkens old sheep runs. Ash and birch clutch the tongue of Childs Hill, once a ledge-y pasture. Where ice and wind have toppled tree trunks over the road, chainsaw shards tell of snowmobilers who have cleared the way for warm-weather dreamers.

At the 1,000-ft. contour, the trees become well spaced and maple now dominates. Below the crest of Childs Hill, an old coot's shack has lain collapsed since Bob Dylan went electric, with a kerosene stove and various mettalica scattered around. And that must be his car too—a '60 Rambler, doors removed, trunk peeled off, and windshield diced by gunfire long since. The engine is out (those thrifty Vermonters), but the driver's vent window still pivots and the cream paint has some-how resisted scores of winters. On the rear bumper is the real object of our affections though: a 1967–68 Dartmouth-student parking sticker, as bright blue as the day it was affixed nearly four decades ago. Perhaps the old coot's place ended its life as a hippie grotto back in the days when Dartmouth grads began to head for local hills, as we do now.

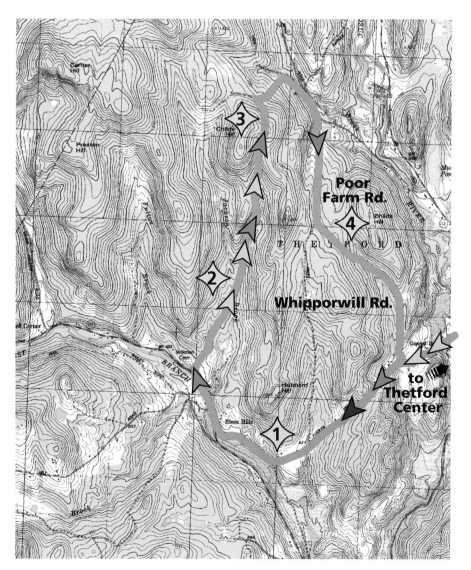

Point of View

As a kid I had a dream I wanted to own a bicycle. When I got the bike I must have been the happiest boy in Liverpool, maybe the world. I lived for that bike. Most kids left their bikes in the backyard at night. Not me. I insisted on taking mine indoors and the first night I even kept it by my bed.

John Lennon

In his classic 1920s monograph *Lyme, A Town That Has Gone Downhill*, geologist James Goldwait managed to blend his training in hard science with a disheartening sociological truth that surrounded him. A good share of the settled landscape of northern New England's youth had been absorbed by the woods.

Lyme had lost half its population over the previous ninety years, as had nearby Orford. But until Professor Goldwait noticed, this drift in human geography had gone unremarked. He decided to investigate just where and how this had happened. Goldwait followed abandoned roads and logging tracks into the blueberry bushes and through snarls of juniper, looking for the remains of what had once been hives of activity during the sheep boom. He determined that the 1,100-foot contour was significant. In the Acorn Hill neighborhood where sixty-nine families once lived in 1825, now only one family lived above that elevation. Twenty-six abandoned houses and cellar holes then lined the Dorchester Road, but only one dwelling was occupied. The newest headstone in the graveyard nearby was dated 1852, but it and thirty-five other lichen-crusted sentinels were embowered in ash and birch.

Goldwait mapped the old roads that had become trails and not the few others that had been lost altogether. Once populated, the shoulders of Smarts Mountain had become simply a blank on government topo maps, he noted, as though nothing had ever happened there. Plott Hill not only had been mostly depopulated, but with no one around to recall its roots had been shorn of a "t" to become plain old Plot Hill.

Cue the Ride . . . The Pinnacle

Lyme 8-mile Loop. From Hanover via River Rd., 32 miles. Moderate difficulty, several walking hills. Paved and dirt. ▬▬▬▬ Hybrid bike, ride clockwise.

Horizon-seekers have been taking in views from the Pinnacle ever since it was cleared for sheep almost two centuries ago. For most of the last century, Camp Pinnacle on Post Pond below would hold a Sunday evening service one night each summer atop it. Boys would hike up for sunset vespers amidst what were then cow pie–dotted open fields. A few lucky ones would sleep the night in the Tip Top House, now burned.

1. Lyme Village Center began to develop about 1810, long after the rest of the town. Porch and interior of Alden Inn of interest.
2. Post Pond, a kettle hole. Formed when an iceberg in a bay of Lake Hitchcock grounded and then was buried in sediment. Eventual melting left depression behind. Footbridge over road once carried boys from Camp Pinnacle to waterfront. Camp, boys, and bridge gone; abutment remains. Note hill profile—The Alligator—across the pond.
3. Whipple Hill Rd. Woodland Indian site, c. 1100–1500 AD, nearby.
4. Path to the Pinnacle, private property that welcomes visitors. Goldwait country lies to the east of the viewpoint.
5. Grafton Turnpike, main road from Quebec to Boston before 1850.

Cue the Ride . . . Plott Hill

Lyme 7-mile Loop. Moderate difficulty, two walking hills. Dirt & paved. Ride counterclockwise. ▬▬▬▬ Use a mountain bike in spring.

This all-to-yourself loop explores a filigree of old roads that are almost unknown except to the people who live on them and perhaps a few deliverymen.

1. Washburn Hill Rd. Short, heavily shaded climb makes for a good walk.
2. Both sides of Plott Hill almost entirely open before 1900. Fence lines still apparent on 1983 edition of topo map. A colonnade of old oaks lines the road.
3. Unmaintained section, mostly a horse road until July. Portion at HOL "paved" with glacially smoothed ledge.
4. Isaac Perkins Rd. loop. Not a soul.

Goldwait's evocative little book is still around in a few libraries and historical associations, and its maps and black-and-white snapshots still fascinate. As suburbanization moves north, the book heads the lists of local titles likely to be reprinted, as it ought to be. Nostalgia has its uses.

Midsummer Eve on the Pinnacle.
Listening for loons on Post Pond below.

Whipple Hill Rd.

Highbridge Rd.

Post Pond

LYME

Acorn Hill Rd.

Washburn Hill Rd.

Lyme Center

Baker Hill Rd.

Lyme Green

One can imagine that in a rural area like the Upper Valley, acquiring an easy-to-ride bicycle in 1895 radically changed one's idea of place. After fifty years of railroading in the valleys, upland towns where the rails didn't go had been left behind and were, perhaps, even more remote than they had been in 1800. Rental carriages from one of the livery stables that operated at every rail depot could get you to Tunbridge or West Newbury, but natural horse power was expensive and sometimes unreliable, and the roads themselves were often in painfully poor condition.

On the other hand, once the newspapers announced the roads were dry, the great outdoors beckoned to young wheelmen and wheelwomen. At the time, it was considered both daring and fashionable to strike out on ambitious journeys all over the New England countryside. Tourers stayed at inns and farmhouses along the way during what was the heyday of Victorian era front-porch tourism. Home stays in the country featured berry picking, rowboats, firefly collecting, and three very large meals a day. When the tour was done or when sheets of rain fouled the roads, wheelers loaded their safety bicycles onto the baggage car at the ever-handy depot down by the river. Almost every town had a bicycle club, usually composed of leading young men and their wives, who organized group tours and maintained a year-round social schedule.

In Hanover, exploits of the cycling Fletcher family give a good idea of how central the bicycle was to activities of the genteel class at the time. The Fletchers lived on North College Street near the White Church, a short but pleasant pedal for Robert Fletcher to his duties as the first director of the Thayer School of Engineering, then on Park Street. Taught to ride a bicycle by his son in 1894, Fletcher soon began making excursions to Norwich, Lebanon and Meriden, frequently accompanied by his daughter Mary. He would often go "awheel" out to Etna, where he was supervising construction work at the Baptist Church, sometimes more than once a day.

Diaries tell us that in July 1898, Robert Fletcher Jr. and a friend cycled to Lake Champlain, returning by train after numerous blowouts. The next day, he and his mother took the train to the Mascoma depot, pedaling back to Hanover via Ruddsboro Rd. As Fletcher Sr.'s diary reports, tire failures were a constant annoyance, once requiring him to walk almost four miles back to Hanover from Norwich, where he had led a student cycling outing. Mechanical repairs were frequent too, but whether breakfast rides, after-dinner rides, or nine-mile rides of an unidentified local "Circuit," nothing deterred the Fletchers. They were crazy for wheeling.

Other than knowing the family was exploring the countryside on one-speeds, the type of machines the Fletchers favored is unrecorded. Advertisements for bicycles began to appear in the *Hanover Gazette* in 1894, when Frost's jewelry store offered the Lovell Diamond brand for cash, on the installment plan, or for rent. In a following issue, high-end manufacturer Pope noted that its "Columbia bicycle is as good as a horse, and much cheaper." By the next season, Norwich merchant L.K. Merrill became the agent for Monarch, "King of All Bicycles," along with models by Templar and Atalanta. Frost countered with Crawford, Hartford, and Iver-Johnson brands, noting the manufacturers he represented were working around the clock to satisfy demand.

In another close parallel to the 1990s, companies created or repositioned a cornucopia of products to be pitched to the needs of cyclists, both real and imagined. Instead of power bars, take liver pills with you on your ride. Instead of Gatorade, drink Hire's Root Beer, "A Beverage for Wheelmen." Instead of spandex shorts, wear bloomers or bicycle suits—"$5 at Sanborn & Co., Lebanon." Whatever it was, in the 1890s if you could tie it to wheeling, you could sell it.

The next novelty, the automobile, appealed to the same craving as the bicycle—freedom of movement. No wonder that as soon as the internal combustion engine patent was broken and autos became cheap, motoring furthered the empowerment of the individual begun by wheeling. How American it all was—and is.

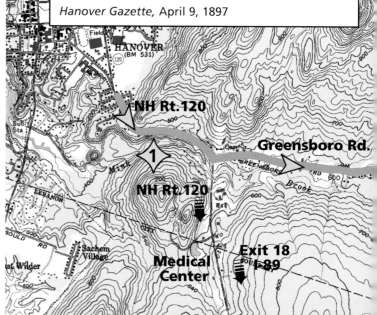

Point of View

Cyclists are impatient at the slowness with which the mud dries up this spring. The Hanover–Norwich Road is all dry except for a short distance on the top of the Norwich hill, and this can be avoided by going through the field to the left.

Hanover Gazette, April 9, 1897

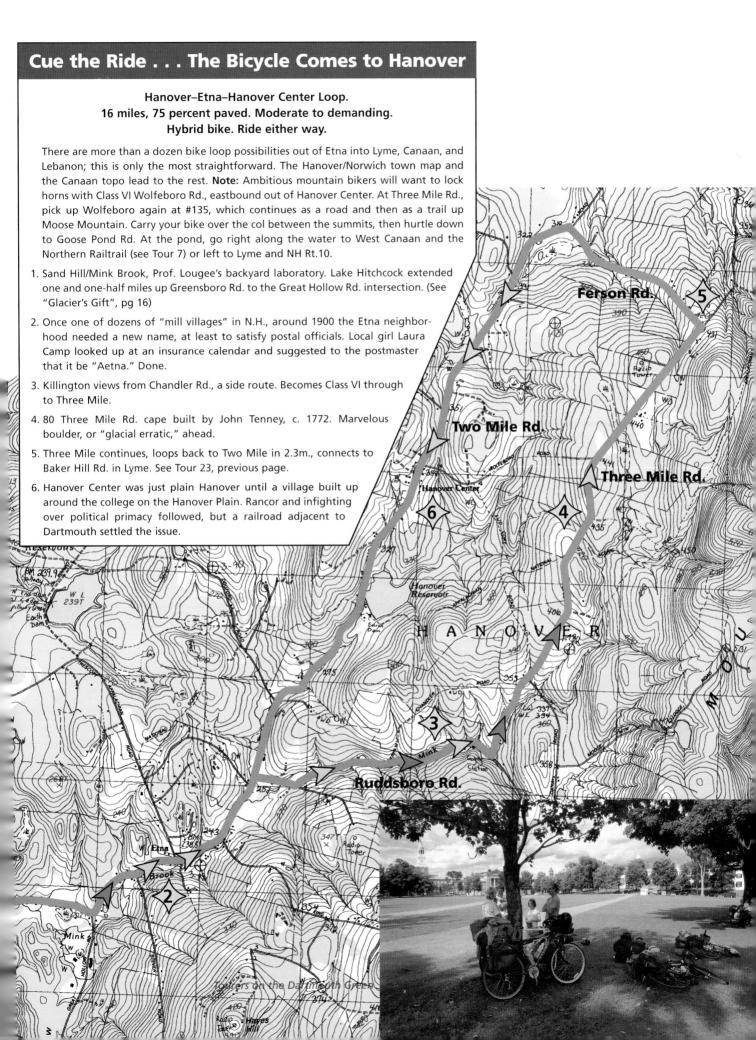

Cue the Ride . . . The Bicycle Comes to Hanover

Hanover–Etna–Hanover Center Loop.
16 miles, 75 percent paved. Moderate to demanding.
Hybrid bike. Ride either way.

There are more than a dozen bike loop possibilities out of Etna into Lyme, Canaan, and Lebanon; this is only the most straightforward. The Hanover/Norwich town map and the Canaan topo lead to the rest. **Note:** Ambitious mountain bikers will want to lock horns with Class VI Wolfeboro Rd., eastbound out of Hanover Center. At Three Mile Rd., pick up Wolfeboro again at #135, which continues as a road and then as a trail up Moose Mountain. Carry your bike over the col between the summits, then hurtle down to Goose Pond Rd. At the pond, go right along the water to West Canaan and the Northern Railtrail (see Tour 7) or left to Lyme and NH Rt.10.

1. Sand Hill/Mink Brook, Prof. Lougee's backyard laboratory. Lake Hitchcock extended one and one-half miles up Greensboro Rd. to the Great Hollow Rd. intersection. (See "Glacier's Gift", pg 16)

2. Once one of dozens of "mill villages" in N.H., around 1900 the Etna neighborhood needed a new name, at least to satisfy postal officials. Local girl Laura Camp looked up at an insurance calendar and suggested to the postmaster that it be "Aetna." Done.

3. Killington views from Chandler Rd., a side route. Becomes Class VI through to Three Mile.

4. 80 Three Mile Rd. cape built by John Tenney, c. 1772. Marvelous boulder, or "glacial erratic," ahead.

5. Three Mile continues, loops back to Two Mile in 2.3m., connects to Baker Hill Rd. in Lyme. See Tour 23, previous page.

6. Hanover Center was just plain Hanover until a village built up around the college on the Hanover Plain. Rancor and infighting over political primacy followed, but a railroad adjacent to Dartmouth settled the issue.

25 Maple Highlands, Hartland

Hotsy-totsy equine pursuits spilled over into Hartland from Woodstock some years ago, and in some ways the little town is a foal of the bigger one. Actress Jill Ireland, late wife of tough-guy film star Charles Bronson, maintained a high-spirited operation on the Barron Hill Road for a time, and swanky horseflesh can still be viewed there from under the shade of ancient roadside maples. But Hartland itself assumes no airs. Natives think of it as a draft-horse kind of place, where live and let live is a way of life—no zoning, police department, or curbside recycling. Overall, it's a precinct of split-personality Vermont. That means

Cue the Ride . . . Maple Highlands Loop

**Hartland, 5 or 10 miles. From Quechee, 16 miles.
Moderate difficulty, rolling climbs. Mostly dirt. Hybrid.**

Note: Lovers Lane and VT Rt.12 make for a pleasant extra spin out to the Four Corners and back from Hartland. Nice barns along the way.

1. Begin in Hartland, a mile off I-91, Exit 9; or Quechee via paved Hartland/Quechee Rd. at blinker light on US Rt.4.
2. Significant climb on dirt Shute Rd. For easier 5-mile loop, go left on Center of Town Rd.
3. 1m. side trip to Talbot's Perennial Farm. Very special irises and such.
4. Mammoth furry Baudette Poitou donkey stud farm. Semen to go, by appointment only. Beaver dam ahead.
5. Bear left on Merritt Rd. Fine views of Ascutney.

as you're peddling from one bump to another along Barron Hill, you'll see rare-breed furry donkeys from France on one side of the road and a beaver dam on the other. Now, if you're from the city you may ask, "How do I tell one from the other?" What an asinine question. As you learned in school, a donkey is not a mule and a beaver is not a rodent. Right?

Speaking of asinine questions, back in the 1920s when it was a dirt road Route 5 in Hartland was the site of the greatest comeback in the history of Vermont humor. As the story goes, a swell in a touring car pulled up at the Three Corners fork, where signs pointing in separate directions each said "White River Jct." Perplexed, the driver hollered to a farmer shoveling manure nearby, "I say, my good man, does it matter which road I take to White River Junction?" Came the reply, "Not to me it don't."

Old Schoolhouse, May, in Hartland

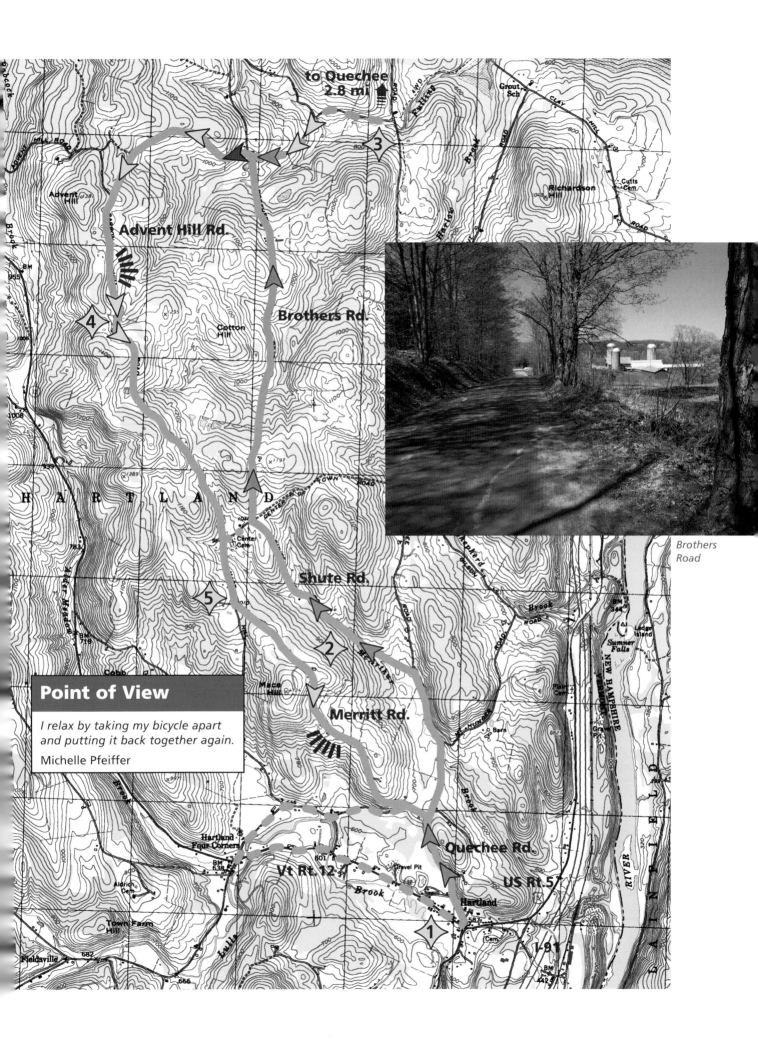

to Quechee
2.8 mi

3

Advent
Hill

Advent Hill Rd.

4

Brothers Rd.

Cotton
Hill

HARTLAND

Brothers
Road

Shute Rd.

5

2

Merritt Rd.

Point of View

*I relax by taking my bicycle apart
and putting it back together again.*

Michelle Pfeiffer

Hartland
Four Corners

Vt Rt. 12

Quechee Rd.

US Rt. 5

Hartland

Town Farm
Hill

1

I-91

Fieldsville

The stony brook that runs along the Beanville Road down into the village of West Fairlee fails to attract much attention from those passing by. (West Fairlee, by the way, is not Fairlee, but a separate town, as anyone from Fairlee will tell you.) Bikers and other explorers following it to Strafford or Vershire may notice the rocks have a certain orange cast to them at low water. But after a mile or so of climbing, glimpses of the brook become few, and the roadside scene—once the local answer to *Deliverance*—gives way to wooded hills. Beanville Road then passes over the Vershire town line and into a valley no different than a hundred others like it in Vermont.

But up ahead, odd-looking debris beside the road gives pause. What are these dump piles full of rubble and bits of old timber, and what's this slag-like material running through it all? On closer inspection, the leavings appear to be just the edge of a large, sour, orange wasteland, trending off in several directions. Stunted poplars, struggling up like big weeds through acres of sandy slag try to disguise the past—but they don't look right. "Popple," as Vermonters call it, invades within a season or two, but cut-stone foundation walls nearby appear to be very old. What, then, is this poisonous mélange the wreckage of? The St. Joseph's Aspirin for Children factory, perhaps?

The weird dumpsite landscape and the sulfate-laden brook running through it are all that survive of Copperfield, one of the largest copper mines in the world in 1880. For decades it flourished as a Nevada-style boomtown of about a thousand residents. During that period, Vershire was to copper what Virginia City was to silver.

Frame boardinghouses and single-family homes stretched for almost a mile along the road, most occupied by hard-rock Irish and Cornish immigrant miners. Churches, stores, a dancehall, even "Photography Rooms" and the Eagle Hotel in West Fairlee served this Roman candle of a community, which flourished for less than forty years. Almost half the population were children, many of whom toiled in the mine. Boys were introduced to work aboveground at the age of ten. After sorting hunks of ore and ringing the bells on tramcars all day, they went to school at night.

The boom had been set off when the Vermont Copper Mining Co. began ore production at the close of the Civil War. When onsite smelting got underway a few years later, mining at Vershire became exceptionally profitable, producing 60 percent of the country's copper. It also became shockingly toxic for the surrounding area. To drive off sulfur, ore was burned on wood piles for months at a time, then finished off in coal-fired ovens. Sulfur dioxide aerosols rising from the smelting operation killed off every green plant within half a mile. One sultry summer afternoon, sulfur vapors were carried to Post Mills, four miles away, where the settling fumes blistered flower and vegetable gardens. The smoking dross from the ovens, which can still be whiffed easily a century later, was simply dumped anywhere handy, usually along the brook. Competition from western copper mines and bad management did Copperfield in, and by 1905 all that remained were rubble piles and deep underground shafts.

VULCAN'S FORGE

Unlike the Elizabeth Mine, with its great plain of unmistakable orange tailings on the New Boston Rd. between South Strafford and Norwich (Tour 20), the more remote Vershire mine was largely forgotten until recently. Thousands of tons of tailings had been hauled off to the Elizabeth smelter in the late 1940s to extract metal that had escaped earlier methods. By that time, the lifeless, miasma-seared hillsides above Copperfield had finally begun to green-up again, although many hardwood species still refuse to grow there today. Some of the miners hung on and found other work, but Copperfield and its associated village of West Fairlee—major American someplaces at one time—had fallen off the face of the earth.

After the mine failed, many of the simple workers' houses sold for $5 and $10 each, usually ending up at Lake Fairlee to be used as camps. The town's two churches were cut up and reassembled miles away in Vershire village. The 700-foot-long sulfur-encrusted smelting

continued, see Tour 27 ⫸

see Tour 27

Beanville Rd.

Vt Rt.113

3

Falls

BM 922

Beanville Rd.

West Fairlee

The workers' town ran along Copper Brook for a mile. Smelter waste was used as fill along its banks.

ROAD

229

Miller Pond Rd.

Camp Kokosing

PODUNK WILDLIFE MANAGEMENT AREA

Miller Pond

BM 1360

Boat Ramp

Copperfield. Vast size of the mine cannot be grasped from the road to South Vershire. This view from the hillside above looks north; road leads to shaft mouth in the distance.

Cooks

4

Maple Hill Rd.

Miller Pond Rd.

to Vt Rt.132 South Strafford

Center Hill

Cue the Ride . . . Copperfield Short Loop

Strafford–S. Vershire–Copperfield.
14 miles, moderate to difficult. Hybrid bike. Ride clockwise.

1. Original Strafford settlement, c. 1768. Small 19th century copper workings farther up Old City Fall Rd.

2. Becomes Vershire Center Rd. at town line near HOL.

3. Copperfield mills and village ran along brook for half a mile. Tramcar line brought ore down from main shaft on the hillside in the site's NW corner.

4. Maple Hill Rd. route includes rough, hilly section. Alternate route via paved Miller Pond Rd. leads to VT Rt.132 (3.8m.), then go right to South Strafford (6.6m.), Strafford (8.5m.). No hills to speak of.

㉗ Copperfield Long Loop

continued from TOUR 26
shed (that's two football fields) eventually burned. Remains that can be located today include cellar holes lining the main street and the mill dam ruins on the brook. Up on the eastern ridge, a massive flue, once connected to the smelter below, yawns to the Vermont skies. From the flue, an eighty-foot chimney spewed fumes downwind for miles around. But you'll need a guide to find these testimonies.

Get a casual look at Copperfield instead by cautiously scrambling down the loose slag slope to the brook on the south side of the road. Each year spring runoff scours out the village's trash heap, unearthing old bottles, blue and white china shards and unknown metal bits that talk of real people. Some of the glass is wilted from molten dross later thrown down on it from the smelter works across the street. Copperfield—sour, scorched land, an Upper Valley ghost town.

ELY MANSION
Architecturally the most memorable structure in town, the Ely Mansion brought $150 at the mine bankruptcy auction. The mansion's builder, a great dandy and the ne'er-do-well grandson of the mine president, dubbed the house Elysium shortly after presenting himself to the world as Ely Ely-Goddard. Artfully relocated at the head of Lake Fairlee, the building's lines—those of a lighthouse keeper's cottage perhaps—grace the waters today better than they ever did a mining camp.

Cue the Ride . . . Copperfield Long Loop

**Strafford–Vershire–W. Fairlee–Copperfield–Campbell Corner.
28 miles, 75 percent paved. Demanding, with three major climbs; for advanced cyclists. Hybrid or road bike. Ride clockwise.**

1. A wonderful paved climb of increasing steepness—or a very long walk.

2. Down, down, down to Brimstone Corner!

3. Copperfield mills and village ran along brook for half a mile. Dirt road leaving right leads to adit in the NW corner of the site, at about the 1,200 ft. level.

4. Return to Miller Pond Rd. to VT132 at Campbell Corner. Turn right there to South Strafford. Also see cues for Tour 26.

ELY DEPOT
Copperfield is also known as the Ely Mine because in 1879, Ely-Goddard, then a state representative and self-styled "colonel," persuaded Vershire voters to rename the town after his family. After abandonment, Ely became Vershire once more. By that time, the railroad siding nine miles away in Fairlee was firmly established as "Ely Station," a name it still holds. Concentrated ore was shipped to Revere, Mass. (remember Revere Ware?) from Ely, but there was never any mining there.

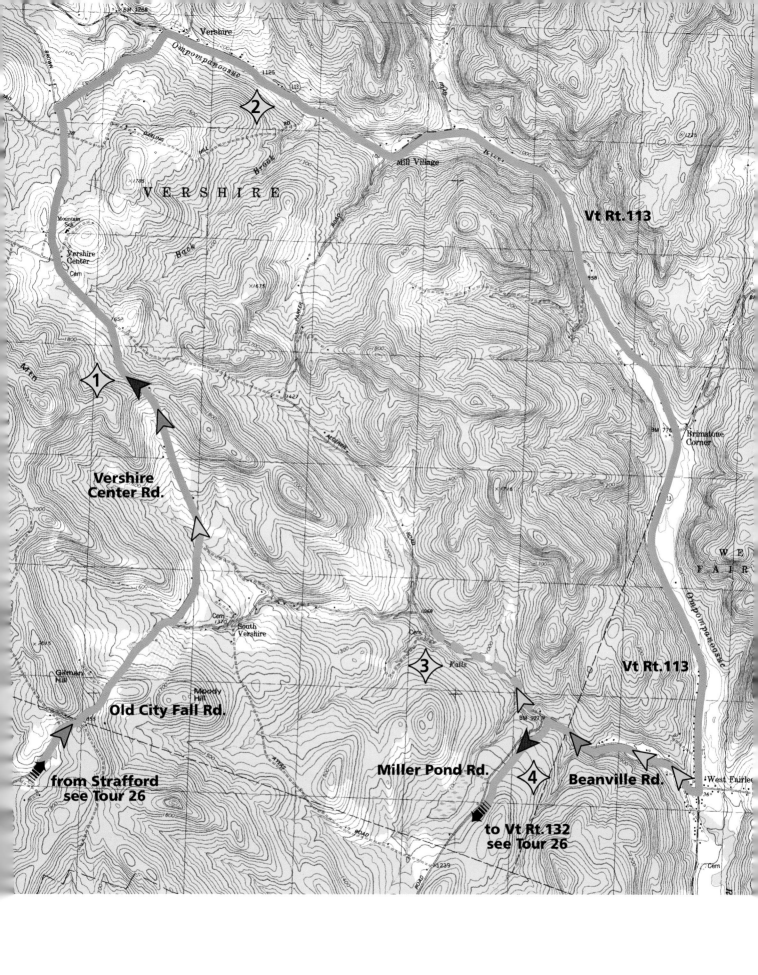

VERSHIRE

Vershire

Ompompanoosue

Mill Village

Vt Rt.113

②

①

Vershire
Center Rd.

Brimstone
Corner

③

Vt Rt.113

Old City Fall Rd.

from Strafford
see Tour 26

Miller Pond Rd.

④

Beanville Rd.

West Fairlee

to Vt Rt.132
see Tour 26

HIS ROUTE RECOUNTED, MILE BY MILE AND MEAL BY MEAL

The Marquis de Lafayette's Grand Tour of the young United States was ten months along when he arrived in central New Hampshire in late June 1824, en route to Vermont. His passage through the Green Mountain State would be remembered by many who witnessed it as the most thrilling day of their lives. Forgotten by 1900, the event was written up on its centenary in local historical society pamphlets and then forgotten once again. What intrigues us now, almost two centuries later, is not only that Lafayette's route between Hartland and Randolph Center is largely intact, but that he might recognize a lot of it.

The Marquis de Lafayette had come north after one of the most important ceremonial duties of his lengthy visit: the laying of the Bunker Hill Monument's cornerstone in Boston. Invited by Congress and then-President James Monroe the previous year, "the Nation's Guest" had already been hosted by sitting President John Quincy Adams at the new White House, conferred with founding fathers Jefferson and Madison in Virginia, laid wreaths at Washington's tomb, and been greeted and feted by tens of thousands in New York and all the mid-Atlantic cities. The purpose in inviting him was to reaffirm the ideals of the new country while some of its founders still lived.

Inordinately affable and unflaggingly enthusiastic, General Lafayette had enjoyed the limelight throughout his sixty-eight years. By the time of his visit, however, his personal circumstances had been greatly reduced by his own revolution and the Napoleonic era that followed. Now he was back in the sun on a tour acknowledged to be a farewell bow to his greatest audience. Among the gifts showered upon Lafayette at every stop by an adoring American public, Congress awarded this living symbol of liberty and nationalism $200,000 in bonds and much of what is now Tallahassee, Florida.

The Marquis had seen much by the time he advanced on the Upper Valley. The previous fall, accompanied by his son

George Washington Lafayette, as well as a secretary and a valet, he had sailed to the Carolinas and Georgia, arduously crossed the backcountry of Florida to Mobile, Ala., and completed his western swing by traveling up the Mississippi to St. Louis. After an early spring side trip to Tennessee to meet General Andrew Jackson, the Ohio River carried his party up to Cincinnati and Pittsburgh, eventually culminating at Buffalo and Niagara Falls in May. Each stop provided occasion for receptions, military revues, parties, banquets, speeches, parades, and honoraria. Now en route to Vermont to place a cornerstone at the new university, Lafayette was wearing his best red wig when his suite departed Claremont, N.H. after breakfast on a warm, overcast Tuesday morning at 7:30. A fifteen-gun salute at the Windsor-Cornish covered bridge was followed by a second breakfast with Vermont Governor Cornelius Peter Van Ness and two hundred others at Pettes Coffee House in town. The dusty streets were packed with some five to eight thousand well wishers, many of whom had held their viewing positions overnight. Pettes later billed the state $166.29 for his services, which included 273 25¢ meals for "solgers."

Six white horses provided by stagecoach magnate Ira Day pulled the general's carriage as it led a procession of dignitaries north from Windsor to Hartland. Via "the hill road," they went on to Woodstock, pausing along Breezy Hill to dispose of a mound of flowers that had risen to the Marquis's knees. "At the foot of the hill at King's Corner," the distin-

May in South Woodstock

guished guest was met and escorted into town by ceremonial militias, rifle companies, and cavalrymen. In Woodstock, words of veneration were uttered from a platform erected in front of Cutting's Hall, about where the library is today. Lafayette then greeted equally aged Revolutionary War veterans in the street on his way to a dinner of roast pig at Barker's Tavern. (Now a stone block, the Barker's location continues to victual visitors, these days as Bentley's.)

August on the Woodstock Green, talking over the ride

After visiting for an hour and a half and changing horses, the party headed north out of Woodstock along the Stage Road through Pomfret to Aikens Stand, a livery in Barnard. There the local artillery company discharged their piece with great fanfare. The whole town had turned out, thanks to Aiken. He was planning to run for the legislature and was giving away free drinks to men with the franchise. Over the hill toward Royalton, the hundred-strong Tunbridge cavalry company, smartly turned out in new crimson coats, joined the carriage column. Mounted trumpeters trotted ahead, blaring the news that the semi-royal train was approaching. Royalton was reached at about 2:00, after a stop at the tollgate. But the stop wasn't to pay the fee, only so the toll collector could offer the honored guests a restorative. At Colonel Smith's Hotel, Jacob Collamer, a future postmaster general under Zachary Taylor, panegyrized at "the thrill of pleasure which, at your condescending visit, vibrates with electric rapidity and sympathetic orison to the most obscure and remote recesses and extremities of our nation." A substantial meal was then laid on atop this filling oratory.

Whether Lafayette actually stopped at the Fox Stand in North Royalton an hour later for a draught of Madeira—or a dose of chalk—as later innkeepers were to claim (à la "Washington slept here"), is not proven. Certainly refreshments would have been at the ready as the cavalcade trotted by, heading toward the second branch of the White River. And certainly remarks were made, hands shaken, and bouquets accepted during another change of teams at East Randolph before the grueling climb to Randolph Center. Once there, Lafayette spoke to large crowds from the porch roof of the three-story brick tavern known as Brackett's Castle. Under his own power, he then reviewed the students of the Orange County Grammar School on Main Street. Details of what food and drink grateful central Vermonters may have offered to the general's continental palate that afternoon have gone unrecorded—mercifully, perhaps.

By 8:00 Lafayette & Co. reached South Barre, and by 9:00 Montpelier, where the Marquis's address to the legislature was followed by a hotel banquet that featured sixteen toasts. Having covered seventy miles of primitive roads in eleven hours in an open carriage, the "Hero of Two Worlds" retired well after midnight, none the worse for his travels, it is claimed. Three months later, he sailed for France on the U.S.S. *Brandywine*, a frigate named for the battle of 1777 in which he was wounded in the leg. The Marquis was accompanied aboard ship by an officer from each of the twenty-four states of the Union. He took with him a chest full of American soil to be spread on his grave. Lafayette died in Paris in 1834.

Cue the Ride . . . Grand Tour

Hartland Four Corners–S. Woodstock–Woodstock. 21 miles., 50/50 paved/dirt. Moderate/difficult, with long walking hills. Plan on a whole day's outing. Hybrid.

One great ride, this. Begin anywhere, ride in either direction; elevation gains are shown going both ways. There are three suggested loops: To follow Lafayette's actual route to Woodstock, start in Hartland and ride counterclockwise, encountering a big hill at the start and then another—after lunch—coming out of South Woodstock. *From* Woodstock, riding in the opposite direction, Hartland Hill Rd. challenges immediately—a mile-long south-facing climb without ten yards of shade. The cues propose a third choice: a clockwise ride from Hartland Four Corners. Choose your poison.

Note: Shorter rides: Hartland Hill Rd./Weed Rd. short loop runs to about seven miles. It may be possible to traverse the ridgeline between Weed Rd. and South Woodstock via the abandoned road to Densmore Cemetery, but that's up in the air.

1. H4C. Talk cycling at Skunk Hollow Tavern, likely the oldest building in town. In former lives, it housed cobbler and butcher shops, a millinery, a dairy drop-off, and a tearoom. Gem of a stone blacksmith shop across the street.

2. Ogden's Mill. Through the 1980s, Herb Ogden spiced up Hartland with a combination wild-apple cider and Deaf Smith Co. organic flour mill, served with a side order of William F. Buckley musings. Much missed.

3. Smoke Rise Farm estate neighborhood.

4. The Loop, high-end side trip. Bikes and horses only, please.

5. South Woodstock reputation for luxe begun by Philly trolley magnate Owen Moon. He assembled 2,000 acres, built a mansion overlooking VT Rt.106 featuring a Greek amphitheater. Estate later became Country School—'70s preppie doper way station. Now it houses the Green Mountain Horse Association, whose red-arrow-on-paper-plate trail markers are everywhere. Vermont Motif #1, the Jenne Farm, can be viewed three miles south on VT Rt.106, just over the Reading line.

6. Hartland Hill Rd. leaves US Rt.4 at CStore conurbation, east of town center. Climb begins with a prodigious walking pitch.

7. Revolutionary War vets buried in Gill Cemetery.

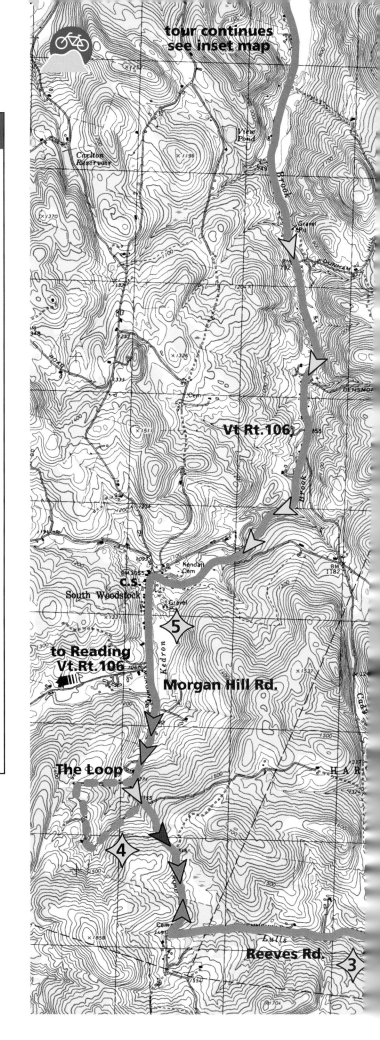

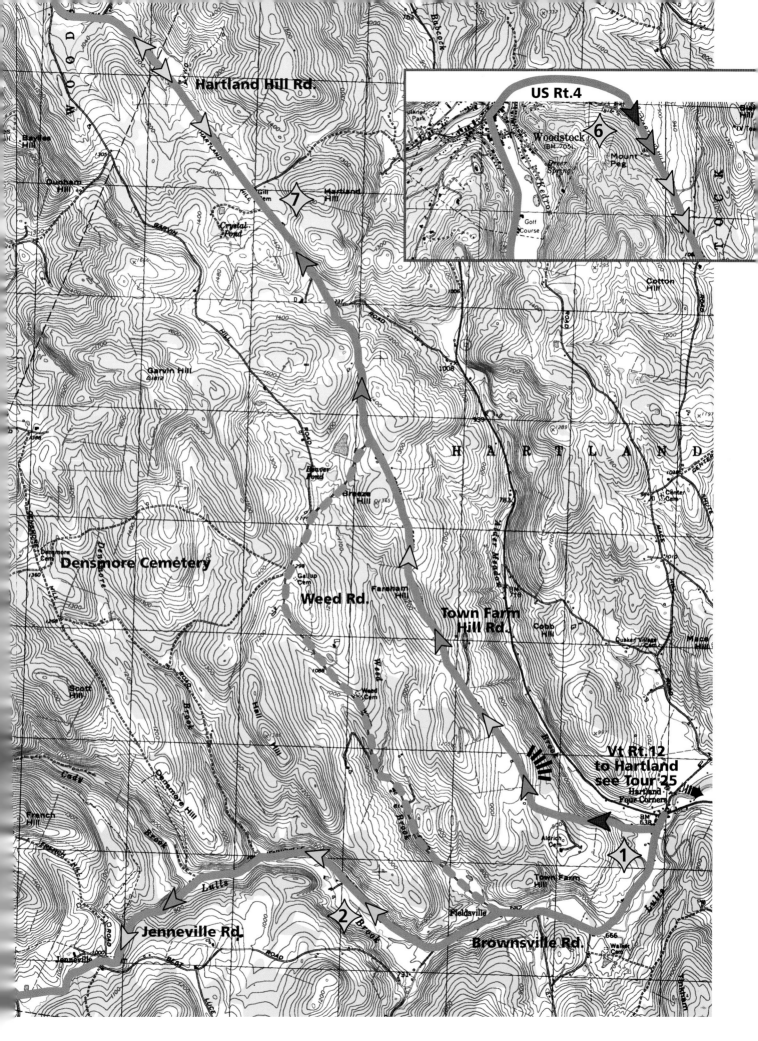

US Rt. 4

Woodstock

Mount Peg

Hartland Hill Rd.

Densmore Cemetery

Weed Rd.

Town Farm Hill Rd.

Vt Rt. 12 to Hartland see Tour 25

Jenneville Rd.

Brownsville Rd.

HARTLAND

29 Ticklenaked to Mosquitoville, The Bayley-Hazen Military Road
Ryegate

When he learned of Benedict Arnold's promising assault on Quebec in the winter of 1776, Col. Jacob Bayley of Newbury sent an urgent dispatch to General George Washington in Philadelphia. I can build a road straight north from the Connecticut Valley to St. John on the St. Lawrence River, he claimed, shortening the supply route to the front by seventy-five miles. Better supplied, the Patriots will surely gain a great victory, giving the Revolution the legitimacy it so sorely needs.

So enthused was Washington by the idea that he forwarded £250 to Bayley by return courier. It was not until two months later that he got around to asking the Continental Congress to approve the scheme. By that time, the route's purpose had regressed to relief of the beleaguered attackers, whose grandiose plan to foment breakaway lust among Canadian provincials had foundered in snowy stalemate.

But public works projects being what they were—and are—opening of the road began early that spring at the head of Main Street. An unnoticed green and yellow metal sign marks the spot. Associates of Bayley had scoped out a route on snowshoes a few months before. Their journal and map of these explorations were the key to piquing strategist Washington's original interest. Gangs of whatever local able-bodied men could be found were hired to fell trees and pull stumps with their oxen. Pay was set at $10 a month, plus all the milk and mush the men could eat and half a pint of Barbados rum a day. By late June, the ancient Indian path and settlers horse trail up the hill from the Connecticut River had been widened to a wagon road of sorts. Its course proceeded on a nearly straight line north through Ryegate, six miles into Peacham. Unfortunately, after Bayley had spent £982 on the effort, news arrived that the siege of Quebec had been abandoned.

From a military standpoint his road was now superfluous, and Bayley was out £700, but he had opened up Ryegate and towns to the north for settlement.

During a second assault on Canada three years later, the Bayley-Hazen Military Road was extended farther north through Cabot and towns beyond, though it never reached the Quebec border. Ironically, the route proved to be of more use to the enemy. Later in the war, British-led Indian raiding parties followed the handy track south, as the settlers of Royalton, tragically, were to learn in the fall of 1780.

The Big Drop to Ticklenaked Pond, Ryegate

Cue the Ride . . . Bayley-Hazen Red Barns Loop

**Ticklenaked Pond–Ryegate Corner–Mosquitoville. 16.5 miles.
From P&H Truckstop, I-91, Exit 17, add 4.6m.
Moderate to advanced difficulty. Hybrid bike.
Ride counterclockwise. No services along this route.**

Note: Unless you enjoy long uphill hikes, forget following the B-H Rd. up from the marker in Wells River. History buffs feeling a need to do so should drive up it instead or bike down it into Wells River from Ticklenaked Pond. Parking is available at the pond boat-launch area.

Accomplished riders can lengthen this outing by beginning at P&H Truckstop, I-91, Exit 17, (homemade bread and humungous pies). Follow US Rt.302 and Boltonville Rd. (See Cross Vermont Trail East, Tour 10.) The 1.5m. climb to Ticklenaked Pond offers a down-sun warm-up for in-shape riders.

This loop can also be enjoyed as the Great Red Barn tour of working, preserved, endangered, collapsed, and lost examples. And save this one for clear weather as it also might be called the Great White Mountain View tour.

1. Ticklenaked Pond. In Abenaki means "place of the beaver."

2. Bayley-Hazen Military Rd. 6.5m. section north to Mosquitoville follows Bayley's original layout almost to the foot.

3. Views to Lafayette Range.

4. Surviving barn on one side of the street, cut stone foundation of a lost companion across the way. Go left on Mosquitoville Rd.

5. Glimpse of Mt. Washington uphill from the barn. Go left on Hall Rd.

6. Hall Farm, 1794 pioneer homestead. Granite from Blue Mt. quarries nearby was a frequent choice for Civil War monuments, including several at Gettysburg.

7. Four Corners. Straight or right leads down to US Rt.302.

to Harveys Lake 1 mi.
to W. Barnet 2.5 mi.

Mosquitoville
Rd.

Hall Rd.

Bayley-Hazen Rd.

Witherspoon Rd.

B-H Rd. South

Boltonville Rd. to
US Rt.302 1.5 mi.

Wells River 4.2 mi.

Daniel Webster arrived in Orford on a late October afternoon in 1840. It was an election year, and Webster had come to talk politics in his old stamping ground. He had been educated at Dartmouth College nearby and had sharpened his incomparable public-speaking skills afterward as a lawyer working in rich towns along the Connecticut, like Orford. By all rights, he should have felt the warm prickle of a homecoming, but the fifty-eight-year-old U.S. Senator from Massachusetts took little pleasure at the prospect of receptions with old friends or the oratory he had come to deliver. He had traveled up to Orford from southern New Hampshire in a half-open barouche, face first into a cold mist. Feverish and distracted from the chilly ride, he soon took to his bed in the Hinckley mansion. (This fine home still stands, second from the north on Bulfinch Row on the luxurious Ridge, painted mid-day yellow today just as it was then.) The house was owned by Edward Bissell, a nephew of inventor Samuel Morey. As the town's leading citizen, Morey had been promoting the development of the Ridge for some thirty-five years as the region's best address.

The next day, perhaps calmed overnight by the restful Rufus Porter murals decorating his chamber, Webster rose from his sickbed. He would fulfill his commitment to address voters on behalf of the odd-couple presidential ticket of Whig William Henry Harrison and Democrat John Tyler. As the man whose rhetoric would later culminate with the deathless "Liberty and Union, now and forever, one and inseparable!" Webster likely attracted a big turnout to the wealthy crossroad that was Orford. Just where he spoke is not known; a likely spot is the second floor porch at the Orford Hotel, burned in 1875, on the north corner of the main and bridge roads. Or perhaps a platform was erected for the event at Willard's Store, then, as now, across the street from the hotel site on the south corner facing the Ridge.

Cue the Ride . . . Indian Pond

Orford–Indian Pond loop. 17 miles, very demanding, major climbs. Hybrid. Ride counterclockwise.

Just as in 1840, Willard's Store in Orford does not offer indoor plumbing. Cyclists are therefore urged to unburden themselves across the river in Fairlee before this very taxing loop of Sunday and Cottonstone Mountains. **Note:** Various routes lead from Orford village to Indian Pond Rd. via (a) NH Rt.25A, or (b) Rt.25A/Dame Hill Rd. at Orfordville, or (c) little traveled Archertown Rd., an "easier" route with only one major climb. Note that "b," the more scenic Dame Hill way, includes a double dip, like riding along the spine of a Bactrian camel; "a" splits the climbing difference. See map and history of the town in *Back in Time*, crackerjack pamphlet from Orford Historical Society.

1. Orfordville, an old mill village. Fine bricks and capes on Dame Hill Rd.

2. Jacobs Brook Rd. Side trip leads to superb swimming along rocky flume a half-mile to the south.

3. Hard, metamorphosed rocks of Sunday and Cottonstone Mts. have resisted erosion longer than surrounding formations.

4. Swimming, canoe launch. No facilities. When Indian Pond Mt. rose as a granite pluton far under the surface during the Mesozoic era, minerals, including gold, were forced into veins in the rock above. Look for flecks in quartz outcrops and pebbly streams in this area that was once known as N.H.'s "mining region."

5. Cole Hill Rd., what dreams are made of. Dirt Class IV, bike/ped only. Autos continue on north to NH Rt.25C in Piermont, then left to NH Rt.10.

After speaking, an anxious Webster consulted a physician summoned by his host. Typical for the times, he was dosed with calomel, a popular all-purpose purgative. Thus unburdened, the following morning he donned a new beaver hat from the local factory and departed for his hometown of Franklin, this time in a closed carriage lent by Bissell.

Indian Pond Road

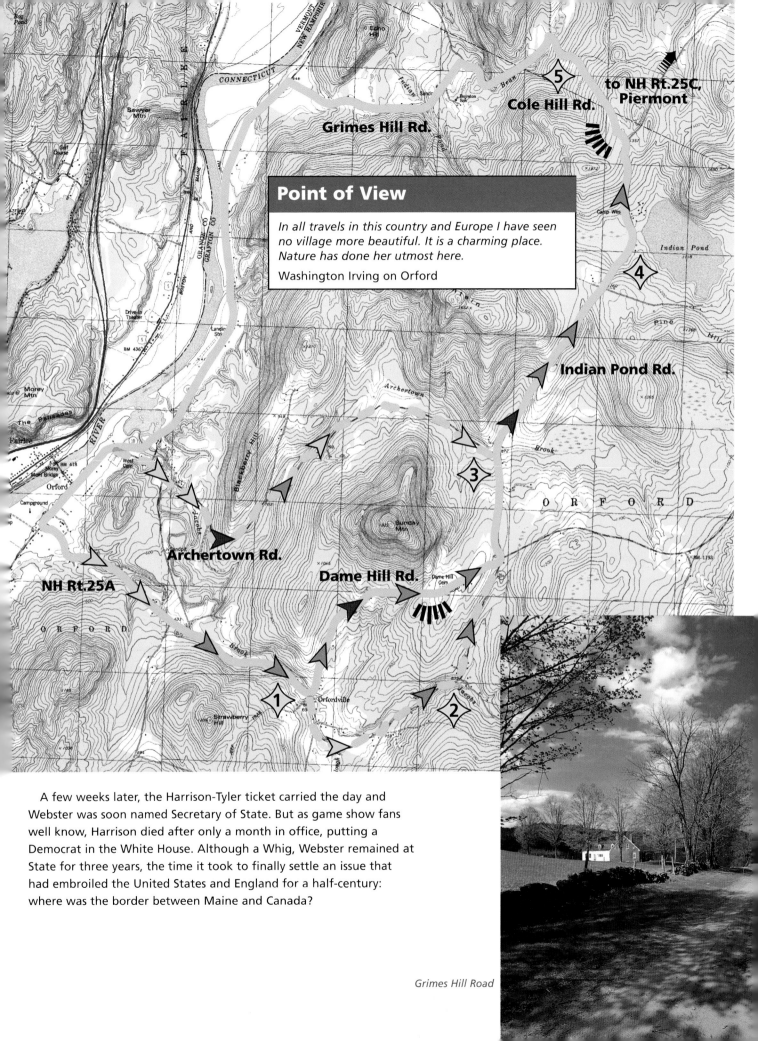

Point of View

In all travels in this country and Europe I have seen no village more beautiful. It is a charming place. Nature has done her utmost here.

Washington Irving on Orford

Grimes Hill Rd.

Cole Hill Rd.

to NH Rt.25C, Piermont

Indian Pond Rd.

Archertown Rd.

Dame Hill Rd.

NH Rt.25A

A few weeks later, the Harrison-Tyler ticket carried the day and Webster was soon named Secretary of State. But as game show fans well know, Harrison died after only a month in office, putting a Democrat in the White House. Although a Whig, Webster remained at State for three years, the time it took to finally settle an issue that had embroiled the United States and England for a half-century: where was the border between Maine and Canada?

Grimes Hill Road

At 1,320 feet, the Pomfret town hall at the top of the pass on County Road has a lot of explaining to do. How did the town come to do its business up here, seemingly way above the human tide line? To begin with, Unitarians presented the hall to the town in 1870 when they were done with it (unity having been achieved, apparently), and that explains a lot but not enough.

The preferred terrain for settlement in the 1700s was uplands, and this is where Pomfret's population used to be. Uphill and south-facing land went dry by May, while valley parcels stayed wet, sometimes all summer. More importantly, because cold air sinks and warm air rises, upland crops were saved from early frosts. Religion was a consideration also. The swamps and thickets of the lowlands gave rise to bad humours and the flux—the devil's work—as was well known. Emotions figured too; on the frontier in 1790 it was comforting to see smoke from neighbors across the valley and know you were not alone. Finally, transcendent ideas affirmed the choice of the highlands: the hilltops were closer to heaven. But, oh, how things changed.

Cue the Ride . . . Pomfret on the Hill

**Woodstock–Pomfret Loop. 18 miles, mostly on hard dirt.
For advanced riders; long, difficult climbs.
Gentrified landscape with numerous views.
Counterclockwise ride suggested. Hybrid or mountain bike.**

1. Cloudland Rd. Half-mile of continually strenuous uphill before HOL at one-room District #2 School, 1797–1954. AT crosses 1.5m. farther along before extra-tough pitch to second HOL. Ahead, exquisite barn with owner who doesn't care for photographers.

2. Forty-two abandoned house sites can be counted on town historian Henry Vail's 1937 map, most around the center of this biking loop.

3. Left at Galaxy Hill gentleman's farm, speedy descent to paved road at ABRUPT T-intersection. Town hall and clerk up the hill. Go left to Webster Hill Rd.

4. Rustic gathering of old roads. Go hard left on Wild Apple Rd., not winter-maintained. Flat mile leads to views, long downhill cruise.

5. Stage Rd. Pres. James Monroe passed by here in 1817 en route to Montpelier. Note stone marking "Edgar Path" opposite, an old woods road/snowmobile trail through maple and beech forest. Makes a nice walk but too steep for bikes.

6. Teago Store. Hotdogs, postcards, post office, *Financial Times*, nice people.

Looking at the current USGS Woodstock North topo, drawn in 1966 at a time when Pomfret was on the cusp of the modern, roads can be picked out of practically every square inch in the V formed by Stage Rd. to the west and County Rd. to the east. But why are there so few little black squares, like Monopoly houses, along what must be a hundred miles or more of traveled way? By the 1960s, the human tide had been ebbing for a hundred years. Half the population that had lived in this ten square miles of "downtown" Pomfret was gone and many of their dwellings had fallen in; more residents could be found in Burns Cemetery than living along all the roads that led to it. Like most other Vermont hill towns, Pontus Fractus—"broken bridge"— had been turned upside down as the gravity of a changing economy tugged farmers and their children downhill, just as it once had the snowmelt from their cobbly fields.

Town Hall, Pomfret

Point of View

It is by riding a bicycle that you learn the contours of a country best, since you have to sweat up the hills and coast down them. Thus you remember them as they actually are, while in a motor car only a high hill impresses you, and you have no such accurate remembrance of country you have driven through as you gain by riding a bicycle.

Ernest Hemingway

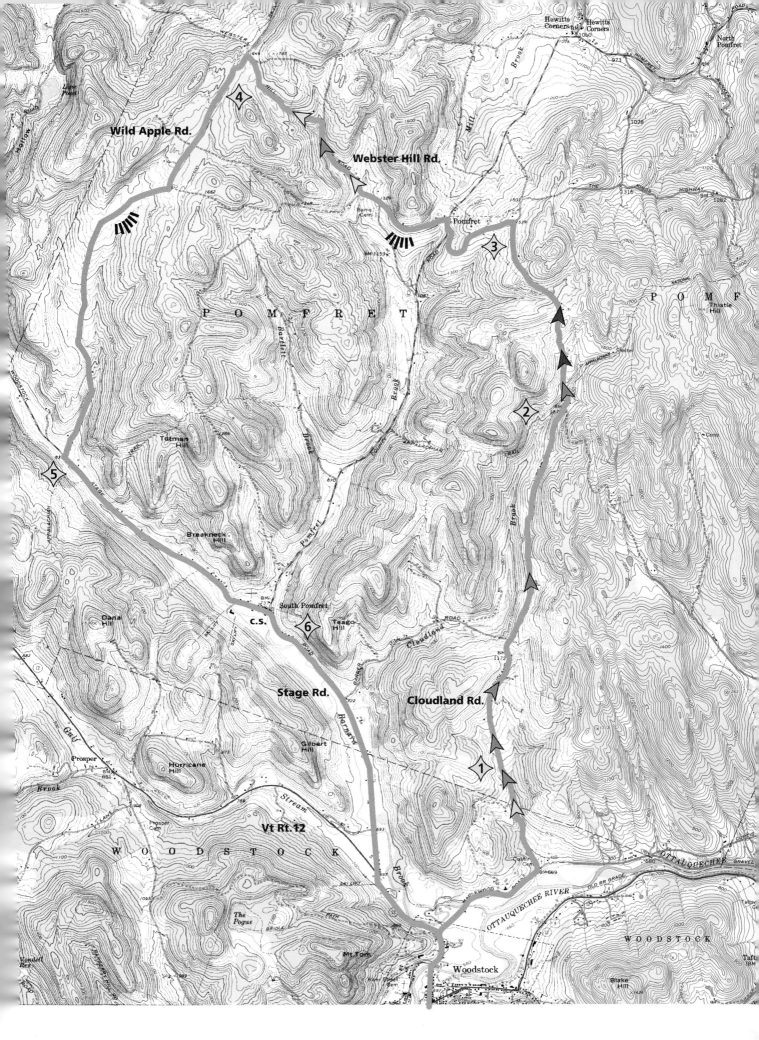

Wild Apple Rd.

Webster Hill Rd.

POMFRET

POMF

Pomfret

3

2

5

Totman Hill

Breakneck Hill

Dana Hill

South Pomfret

C.S.

6

Teago Hill

Stage Rd.

Cloudland Rd.

Prosper

Hurricane Hill

Gilbert Hill

1

Vt Rt. 12

WOODSTOCK

The Pogue

Mt Tom

Woodstock

WOODSTOCK

OTTAUQUECHEE RIVER

Blake Hill

32 Kings Highway
Quechee-Pomfret

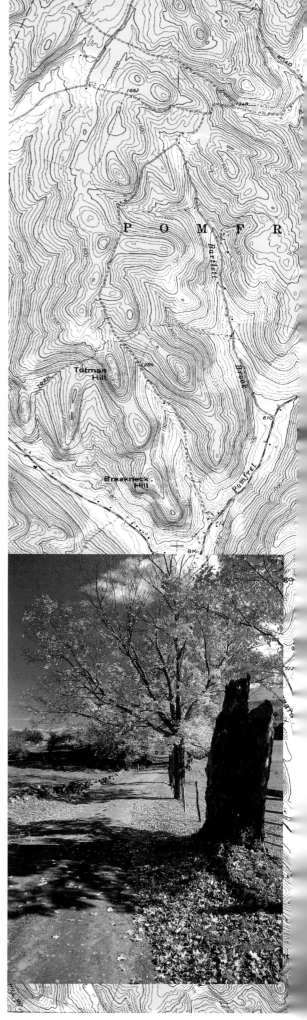

Cue the Ride . . . Kings Highway

Quechee–Pomfret–Quechee Loop.
17 miles, very demanding, numerous climbs. Mostly dirt.
Hybrid or mountain bike.

Thousands of acres of Quechee farmland and second-growth woods were quietly bought up by a visionary Andover, Mass., developer in the 1960s for $50–$100 an acre, thrilling town of Hartford taxpayers no end when they heard of it. Until then, the neighborhood was thought of mostly as the host of the "Poor Farm" and the vacant woolen mills that had gone over the dam in the 1950s. Since the development's inception, a half-dozen different entities—from Big Board insurance companies to future jailbirds—have sold lots and condos at Quechee Lakes. Actually, there's only one lake, Plastic Pond, named for the material that holds in the water.

A tour from Quechee through Pomfret and back again provides a pedal through Vermont's past and present for visitors. In the village, inns and B&Bs recall old-fashioned front porch tourism. Up in Pomfret, the self-aware perfection of the Galaxy Hill estate area speaks of the idealization of Vermont by the wealthy from downcountry. A little farther on, except for the cattle being raised for meat instead of milk, the farm scene at the corner of Galaxy Hill and Kings Highway appears much as touring-car riders would have seen it in 1925. But at the summit of Joe Ranger Rd. on Bunker Hill, old cellar holes, once entirely antique in their effect, now accessorize a McMansion subdivision. This is distressing, all right, but some comfort can be gained by knowing the original '80s developer, who mulcted a Rutland bank to finance it, did time in a federal pokey for doing so. Abandoned Vermont can be viewed at the foot of Joe Ranger Rd., where the sinking roof lines of shed and barn complex define wrack and ruin. But hurry.

Park at the Green in the village, at the Gorge, or around the golf course. Clockwise ride recommended. Take double water; no services along the way. To take this tour by car, use Cloudland Rd. to Galaxy Hill. See Tour 31.

1. Start. Quechee Village is one mile east. Follow River Rd.

2. Hillside Rd., hard dirt. Moderate, then easier climbing. Becomes Spalding Lane, follows route cut by Pomfret proprietors in 1770 to get to their township.

3. Town road becomes woods road. Pass under power line, up, over, and down to Cloudland Rd. Ascutney view.

4. AT crosses, extra-tough pitch to HOL.

5. Right on Galaxy Hill Rd. at estate area. Becomes Kings Hwy. after downhill through sugarbush. Not winter maintained for .8 miles.

6. Long-distance easterly views to Jericho neighborhood of Hartford. Bare summit to the right is Cardigan Mt. in N.H.

7. House with gazebo-like porch was town Poor Farm. Views.

Old Kings Highway, Pomfret

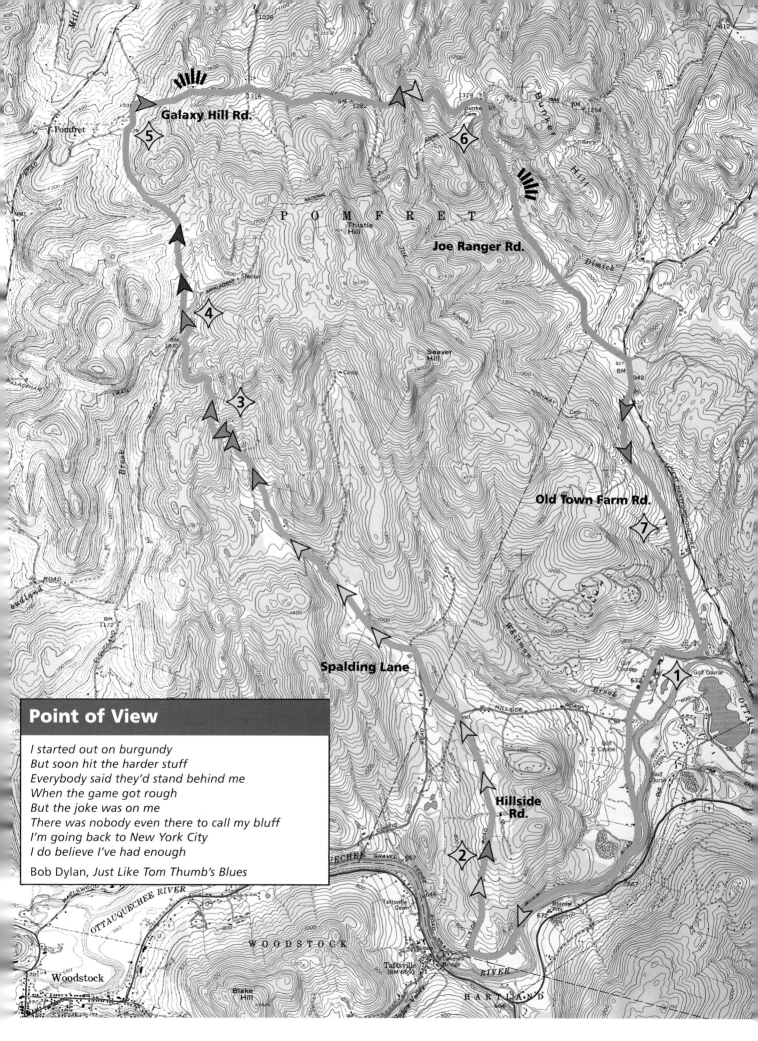

Galaxy Hill Rd.

5

Joe Ranger Rd.

6

4

3

Old Town Farm Rd.

7

Spalding Lane

1

Hillside Rd.

2

Point of View

I started out on burgundy
But soon hit the harder stuff
Everybody said they'd stand behind me
When the game got rough
But the joke was on me
There was nobody even there to call my bluff
I'm going back to New York City
I do believe I've had enough

Bob Dylan, *Just Like Tom Thumb's Blues*

WOODSTOCK

Woodstock

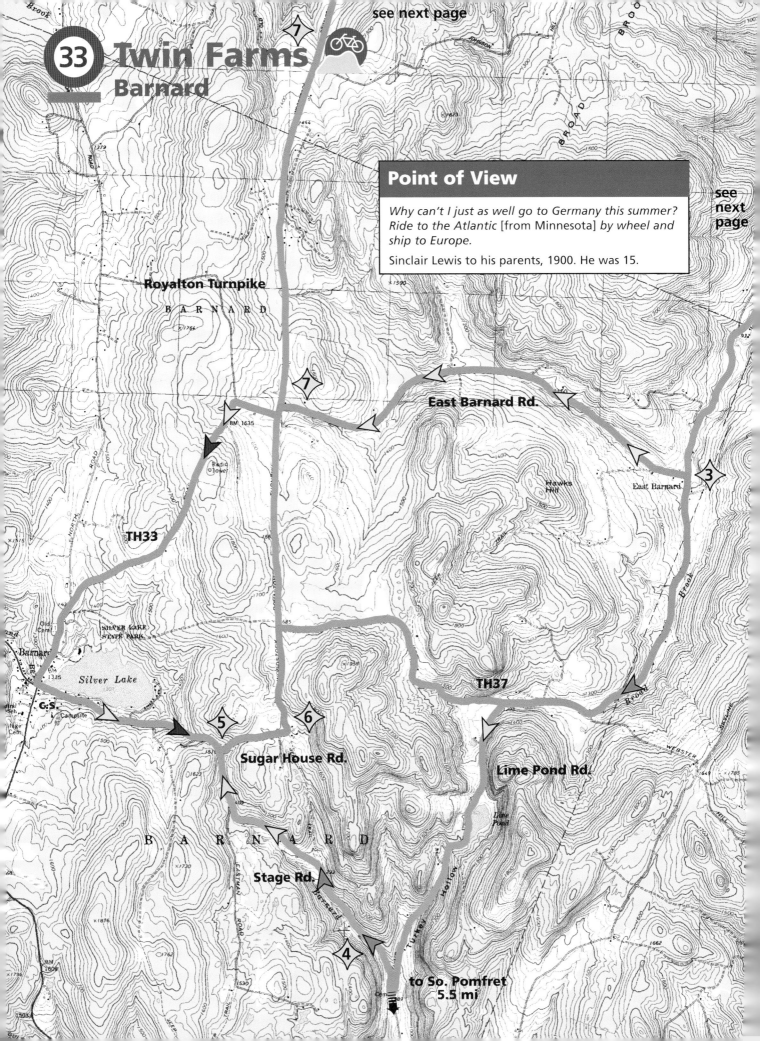

33 **Twin Farms**
Barnard

see
next
page

Point of View

Why can't I just as well go to Germany this summer?
Ride to the Atlantic [from Minnesota] *by wheel and*
ship to Europe.

Sinclair Lewis to his parents, 1900. He was 15.

Royalton Turnpike

B A R N A R D

East Barnard Rd.

East Barnard

TH33

Hawks
Hill

Silver Lake
State Park

Barnard

Silver Lake

G.S.

TH37

Sugar House Rd.

Lime Pond Rd.

B A R N A R D

Stage Rd.

to So. Pomfret
5.5 mi

Cue the Ride . . . Twin Farms

Barnard–East Barnard Loop. 10 miles, moderate. Walking hills.

Barnard has plenty of good biking roads but no road signs. Theft doesn't seem to be the problem since thieves don't usually steal the poles too. Apparently, like southern England in 1940, the town expects a (second) German invasion sometime soon. Small "TH" (town highway) signs show up attached to speed limit signs here and there, but don't count on finding a lot of them. Instead, ask passersby, but not people driving large Mercedes and BMWs. They're looking for Twin Farms and are lost themselves.

From Silver Lake a suggested ten mile ride follows Stage Rd. east to Twin Farms (Tour 34, Cue 6), then north on the Turnpike to TH37. Make a counterclockwise loop from there to East Barnard, returning to the Turnpike via East Barnard Rd. Tough TH33 is optional.

Note: There are no cues for Tour 33. Cues refer to Tour 34, next page.

Within a few days of meeting each other in 1927, America's most famous novelist, Sinclair Lewis, and America's leading foreign correspondent, Dorothy Thompson, agreed that if they should marry, they would buy a farmhouse somewhere in the New England countryside. Lewis even sketched out its shape and forecast that it would look down a valley. While motoring through Vermont in September of the following year, the newlywed couple dropped in on their Manhattan landlord at his summer place, Twin Farms, in Barnard. Within a few hours, they had bought the property—two houses and 300 acres—for $10,000 even, taking possession the next day. As foretold, Twin Farms overlooked the vale of Barnard Brook.

In the years that followed, Lewis would win the Nobel Prize for *Main Street, Babbitt, Elmer Gantry*, and other works. Thompson would be kicked out of Germany for reporting on the rise of the Nazis. And while both would continue to hit the typewriter hard, she would also take to the country with gusto, pouring money into the houses, grounds, and environs. She quickly became a Vermont celebrity for the finest formal garden in the state, for reams of traffic tickets, and for buying up property all over town and in Woodstock. Today her legacy is her 1930s role as a primary liaison for German-speaking émigrés trying to escape Mittel-Europa. According to biographer Peter Kurth, at a time of strict immigration controls and anti-foreigner sentiments, Thompson ceaselessly besieged authorities on behalf of persecuted Europeans who needed documents. By this time, she was America's most read newspaper columnist and had great leverage in Washington. Her persistence often paid off, and within a few years the droll Lewis began to call his part of the state Mittel-Vermont.

Refuge seekers with names like Zuckmayer (novelist and playwright), Shwarzenberg (princess), Bruning (last German democratic chancellor), Rosenstock-Huessy (legal historian, philologist), and Rothschild (one and the same) filled the streets of Woodstock, often wearing lederhosen and dirndls on Saturdays. At one point, Lewis asked petulantly, "Does anybody at Twin Farms speak English anymore?" As the years went by, émigrés filtered out from Barnard to towns nearby, with academics trending toward Norwich and Hanover.

In 1942 Dorothy Thompson was granted a divorce from Lewis at the Woodstock courthouse on grounds of desertion, gaining Twin Farms as part of the settlement. The all-American novelist and world-class boozehound would die eight years later, while Thompson would continue to maintain Barnard as a crossroads for intellectuals and artists from around the world. But times changed. In winter 1959, she took an apartment at 26 East Wheelock St. in Hanover, imagining she might become a literary hostess. Her foray was a failure, as Dartmouth undergraduates had only a vague notion of who she was. When she died in 1961,

Thompson was hailed as the greatest woman journalist of her day. She is buried next to her third husband, sculptor Maxim Kopf, in the Barnard cemetery.

Twin Farms was sold to Hans Kurach, a Swiss, in 1966. He cut ski trails and installed a lift, operating the property as an old-fashioned ski area called Sonnenberg. The smaller of the two houses burned in the 1980s. By then the estate was owned by the Twigg-Smith clan, who had purchased it as a summer place. Twin Farms was converted to an ultra-luxe resort in the '90s. The job was financed by the sale of the *Honolulu Advertiser*, the Twigg-Smith family's holding, which dated back to ancestors who had gone out to Hawaii as missionaries. Nine cottages are now sprinkled about the grounds, a few of which are visible by peering through the security gates and across the helipad. These days twenty thousand gets you the run of twinfarms.com for a whole day, mountain bikes included. Thompson would probably raise a glass of champagne to all of this, with a special toast to the flower gardens.

Québecois picnicking at Silver Lake.

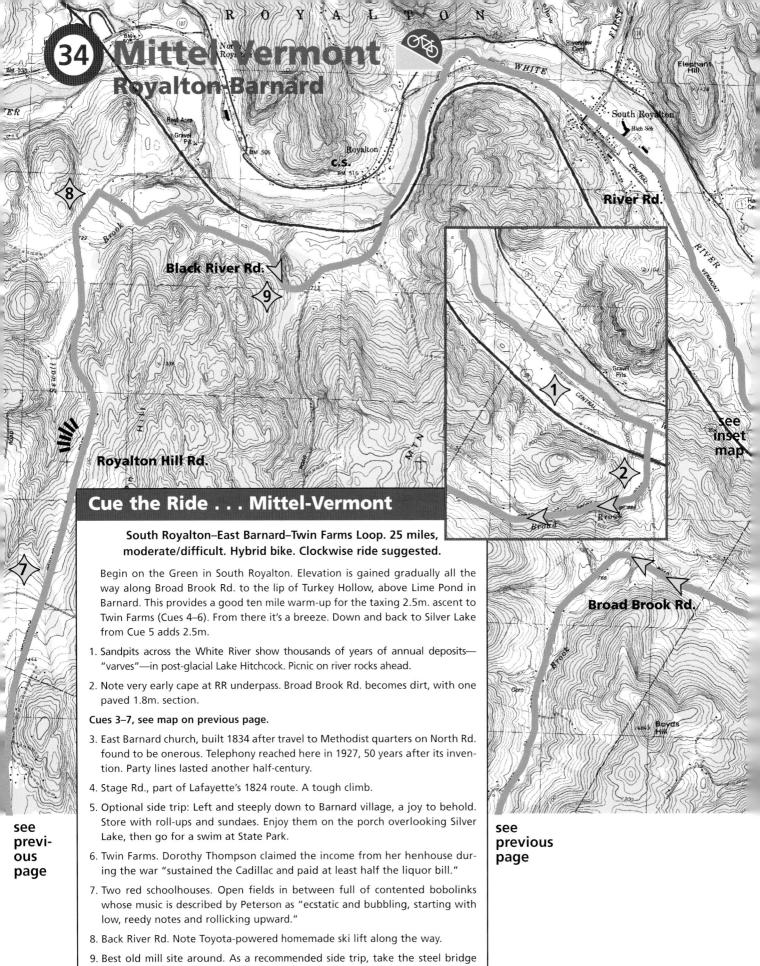

Black River Rd.

River Rd.

Royalton Hill Rd.

see inset map

Broad Brook Rd.

Cue the Ride . . . Mittel-Vermont

South Royalton–East Barnard–Twin Farms Loop. 25 miles, moderate/difficult. Hybrid bike. Clockwise ride suggested.

Begin on the Green in South Royalton. Elevation is gained gradually all the way along Broad Brook Rd. to the lip of Turkey Hollow, above Lime Pond in Barnard. This provides a good ten mile warm-up for the taxing 2.5m. ascent to Twin Farms (Cues 4–6). From there it's a breeze. Down and back to Silver Lake from Cue 5 adds 2.5m.

1. Sandpits across the White River show thousands of years of annual deposits—"varves"—in post-glacial Lake Hitchcock. Picnic on river rocks ahead.

2. Note very early cape at RR underpass. Broad Brook Rd. becomes dirt, with one paved 1.8m. section.

Cues 3–7, see map on previous page.

3. East Barnard church, built 1834 after travel to Methodist quarters on North Rd. found to be onerous. Telephony reached here in 1927, 50 years after its invention. Party lines lasted another half-century.

4. Stage Rd., part of Lafayette's 1824 route. A tough climb.

5. Optional side trip: Left and steeply down to Barnard village, a joy to behold. Store with roll-ups and sundaes. Enjoy them on the porch overlooking Silver Lake, then go for a swim at State Park.

6. Twin Farms. Dorothy Thompson claimed the income from her henhouse during the war "sustained the Cadillac and paid at least half the liquor bill."

7. Two red schoolhouses. Open fields in between full of contented bobolinks whose music is described by Peterson as "ecstatic and bubbling, starting with low, reedy notes and rollicking upward."

8. Back River Rd. Note Toyota-powered homemade ski lift along the way.

9. Best old mill site around. As a recommended side trip, take the steel bridge ahead across the White River to Royalton.

see previous page

see previous page

(35) Target of Opportunity
Royalton

Attacked by British-led Indians during the revolution, Royalton was an unlucky target of opportunity rather than a site chosen for its military value. The force of three hundred raiders that made it famous initially planned to savage Newbury on the Connecticut instead. Their goal was to terrorize the burgeoning Coos countryside and to take prisoners back to Quebec and hold them for ransom. The Brits also had their eye out for a certain Major Benjamin Whitcomb, who a spy had reported was on duty at Newbury. His kidnapping was to avenge British honor, which Whitcomb apparently had wounded earlier in the war.

Setting from Lake Champlain with this well-laid plan in mind, the war party came upon and captured some Newbury men hunting near what is now Montpelier. Don't bother going to our hometown, the king's men were advised. Our hero, Col. Jacob Bayley (see Tour 29), has heavily defended the riches of the Oxbow with a blockhouse and guards on patrol 24/7. Whitcomb? Never heard of him.

Swallowing this fish story whole, the British commander sent his scouts south along the First Branch of the White River to find an alternate victim. Little Royalton was unready though not, it seems, unaware of the threat. Two months before, a small force of Indians attacked nearby Barnard and three men had been abducted. At Royalton, a strongpoint of logs called Fort Fordway had been built sometime before the Barnard raid on the south bank of the river, near where the high school is today. But the fort had been disassembled for its lumber that spring and not rebuilt. Otherwise, the settlement was little more than a scattering of homesteads along the rocky White River and had no village center to assault nor obvious wealth to speak of.

No warning came, and at first light on October 4, 1780, farmers and their families awoke to the terror of tomahawk-wielding "devils" appearing from nowhere. Men running for the woods were hacked to death. Women and children were subdued and herded to assembly points manned by officers. Most livestock was simply slaughtered. Intent on finding jewelry and silver, the Indians then ransacked the houses, setting them afire afterward.

A few people escaped at the launching of the onslaught, which began near the Tunbridge town line. The lucky few rode or ran downstream along the First Branch, screaming warnings to their neighbors as they raced by. Joseph Parkhurst alerted Elias Stevens, already in the fields with his oxen collecting pumpkins. Stevens took a horse downriver, sounding the alarm. Many whom he aroused successfully took flight, as the Indians behind paused to plunder. Phineas Parkhurst, Joseph's brother, was fleeing across the White near the Sharon town line when shot by an Indian from the riverbank above. The musket ball lodged under the skin of his chest, but he rode on fifteen miles downstream to warn Hartford before taking himself to a doctor in Lebanon.

Over several hours, the raiders torched houses, barns, and mills along six miles of the White River, between the mouth of the second branch (North Royalton) and Broad Brook in Sharon. Although mothers begged the English to leave behind their younger children, twenty-six settlers of all ages were driven north toward Randolph. That night, a poorly organized and ineffectual militia of several hundred local men pursued the marauders, skirmishing briefly with a rear guard near Brookfield. The ill-fated rescue prompted the Indians to abandon a number of stolen horses, making the journey to Canada all the more difficult for their captives. Several died en route; others were sold in Montreal for $8 each. Most did return years later, among them one Zadoch Steele, whose account tells the tale. **Map & Cue 35 on next page ▶**

> ### Point of View
>
> *There are about ninety-one miles of public highway in town, not counting pent roads. The roads are probably in better condition than they ever were before. The two main roads on either side of the river and the Chelsea road are much frequented by autos, and no more beautiful drives can be found anywhere, than in following the sinuous courses of the river and the two branches, with their green islands and tree-bordered banks, and letting the eye delight in the forest-crowned hills that feed these lovely streams. There is an auto station at South Royalton near the new iron bridge . . . and the village welcomes the weary and hungry traveler, and sends him on his way with pleasant recollections of the beautiful, old historic town.*
>
> Evelyn Lovejoy, *History of Royalton*, 1911

South Royalton

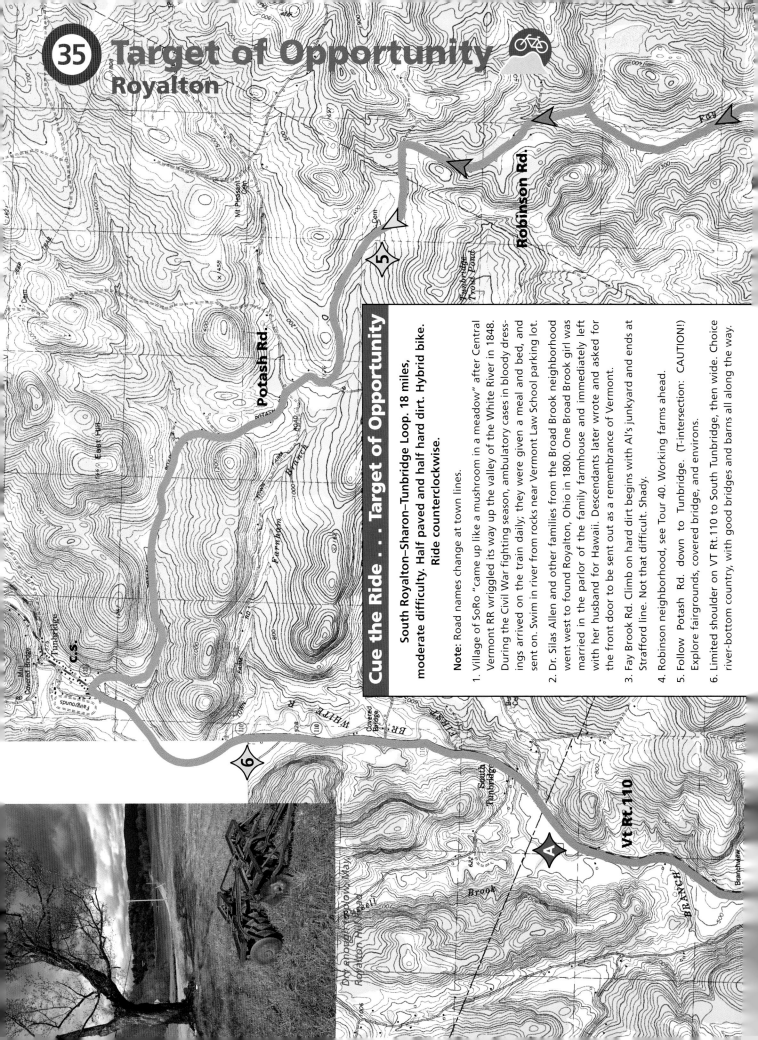

35 Target of Opportunity
Royalton

Cue the Ride . . . Target of Opportunity

South Royalton–Sharon–Tunbridge Loop. 18 miles, moderate difficulty. Half paved and half hard dirt. Hybrid bike. Ride counterclockwise.

Note: Road names change at town lines.

1. Village of SoRo "came up like a mushroom in a meadow" after Central Vermont RR wriggled its way up the valley of the White River in 1848. During the Civil War fighting season, ambulatory cases in bloody dressings arrived on the train daily; they were given a meal and bed, and sent on. Swim in river from rocks near Vermont Law School parking lot.

2. Dr. Silas Allen and other families from the Broad Brook neighborhood went west to found Royalton, Ohio in 1800. One Broad Brook girl was married in the parlor of the family farmhouse and immediately left with her husband for Hawaii. Descendants later wrote and asked for the front door to be sent out as a remembrance of Vermont.

3. Fay Brook Rd. Climb on hard dirt begins with Al's junkyard and ends at Strafford line. Not that difficult. Shady.

4. Robinson neighborhood, see Tour 40. Working farms ahead.

5. Follow Potash Rd. down to Tunbridge. (T-intersection: CAUTION!) Explore fairgrounds, covered bridge, and environs.

6. Limited shoulder on VT Rt.110 to South Tunbridge, then wide. Choice river-bottom country, with good bridges and barns all along the way.

Robinson Rd.

Potash Rd.

VT Rt.110

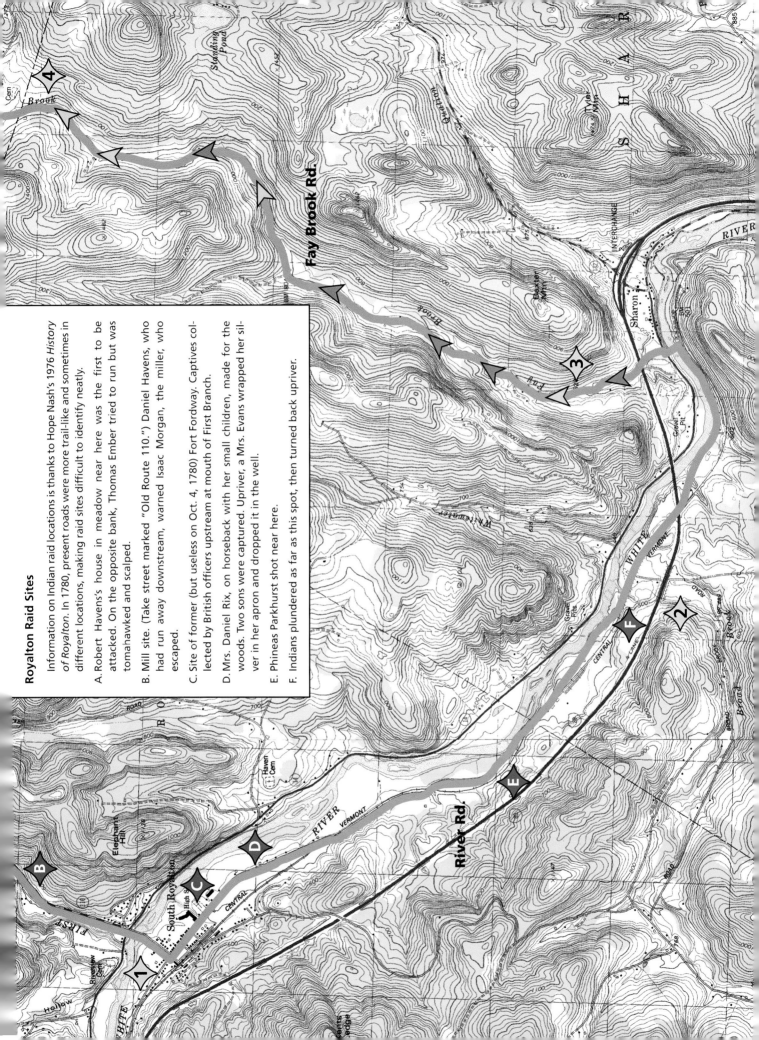

Royalton Raid Sites

Information on Indian raid locations is thanks to Hope Nash's 1976 *History of Royalton*. In 1780, present roads were more trail-like and sometimes in different locations, making raid sites difficult to identify neatly.

A. Robert Havens's house in meadow near here was the first to be attacked. On the opposite bank, Thomas Ember tried to run but was tomahawked and scalped.

B. Mill site. (Take street marked "Old Route 110.") Daniel Havens, who had run away downstream, warned Isaac Morgan, the miller, who escaped.

C. Site of former (but useless on Oct. 4, 1780) Fort Fordway. Captives collected by British officers upstream at mouth of First Branch.

D. Mrs. Daniel Rix, on horseback with her small children, made for the woods. Two sons were captured. Upriver, a Mrs. Evans wrapped her silver in her apron and dropped it in the well.

E. Phineas Parkhurst shot near here.

F. Indians plundered as far as this spot, then turned back upriver.

36 Peaceable Kingdom
Bethel-Randolph

Cue the Ride . . . Peaceable Kingdom

North Royalton–East Bethel–Randolph Center Loop.
21 miles, very difficult climbs. Paved and dirt. Hybrid or road bike.

Miraculously bypassed by both the railroad and the interstate, the valley of the Second Branch of the White River delights, with fifteen miles of pre-1840 fossils at every bend in the road. There are no easy routes from the valley to Randolph Center, seven hundred feet above. The preferred choice, dirt Silloway Rd., requires a full half-mile of hiking at the bottom and two other significant walking hills farther on. But it presents superior architecture, views, and shade. Other routes are merely stunning.

1. I-89, Exit 3. Park. Before the ride, feast on pancakes at the Sugar House.
2. Splendid octagon schoolhouse retains original child-proof Smith patent woodstove.
3. Alternate route to Randolph Center via dirt Crocker Rd.
4. Spectacular brick tavern, c. 1815; a relic of the stagecoach era, in need of immediate preservation.
5. VT Rt.66 paved alternative to Randolph Ctr. for road bikers. Unremittingly steep, little shaded, suitable for Tour de France training.
6. Ridge Rd., paved/dirt. One mile to panoramic southerly views of Killington. Unique Floating Bridge, 5m. ahead over hill and dale at Brookfield.
7. East Bethel Rd. bears right at Y. Use caution at asphalt/dirt transition.
8. Stopped-in-time hamlet, once home to stonecutters who quarried granite from ledges high on Quarry Hill above. Beers 1869 Atlas shows hotel, three dry goods stores, a tin shop, tub factory, and a "BS Shop."

Point of View

The small Vermont house, left without its barns and sheds, has had a hard time. Some of the big fine houses have also been neglected and mistreated, but at least some people notice and regret it.

Royalton Vermont, Hope Nash

*June,
Town Highway 3,
East Bethel*

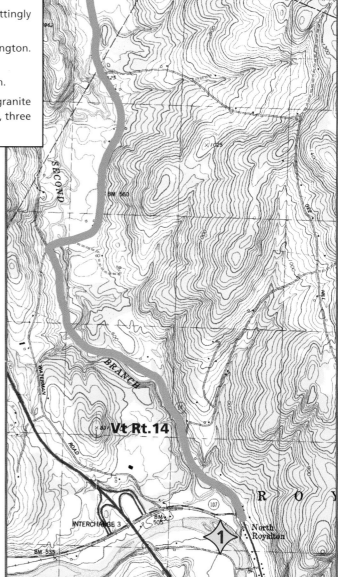

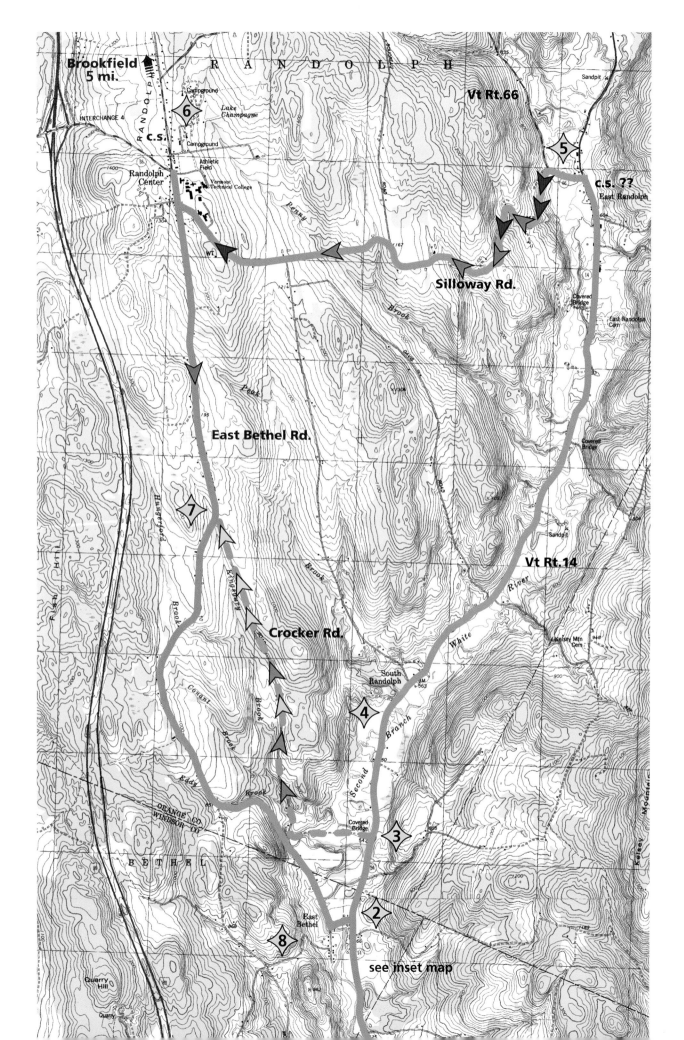

Brookfield
5 mi.

R A N D O L P H

Vt Rt.66

INTERCHANGE 4

6

c.s.

Campground

Lake
Champagne

Campground

Athletic
Field

Randolph
Center

Vermont
Technical College

5

C.S. ??

East Randolph

Silloway Rd.

Covered
Bridge

East Randolph
Cem.

Peak

East Bethel Rd.

7

Covered
Bridge

Vt Rt.14

Sandpit

Crocker Rd.

South
Randolph

Kelsey Mtn
Cem

4

3

Covered
Bridge

ORANGE CO.
WINDSOR CO.

B E T H E L

East
Bethel

8

2

see inset map

Quarry
Hill

Quarry

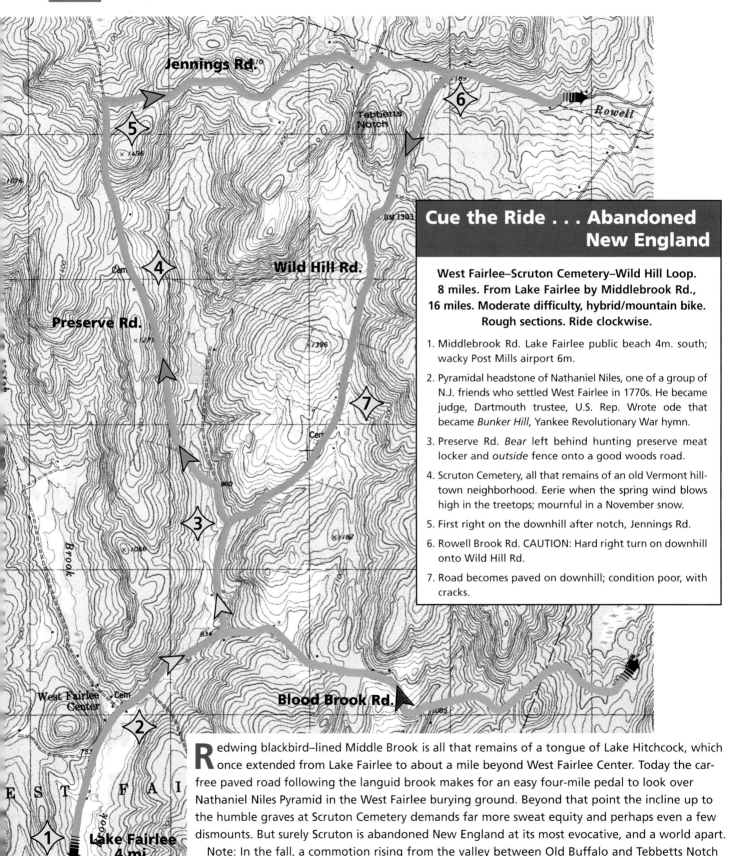

Jennings Rd.

5

Tebbetts Notch

6

Rowell

4

Wild Hill Rd.

Preserve Rd.

7

3

Blood Brook Rd.

West Fairlee Center

2

WEST FAI

1 Lake Fairlee 4 mi.

Cue the Ride . . . Abandoned New England

**West Fairlee–Scruton Cemetery–Wild Hill Loop.
8 miles. From Lake Fairlee by Middlebrook Rd.,
16 miles. Moderate difficulty, hybrid/mountain bike.
Rough sections. Ride clockwise.**

1. Middlebrook Rd. Lake Fairlee public beach 4m. south; wacky Post Mills airport 6m.

2. Pyramidal headstone of Nathaniel Niles, one of a group of N.J. friends who settled West Fairlee in 1770s. He became judge, Dartmouth trustee, U.S. Rep. Wrote ode that became *Bunker Hill*, Yankee Revolutionary War hymn.

3. Preserve Rd. *Bear* left behind hunting preserve meat locker and *outside* fence onto a good woods road.

4. Scruton Cemetery, all that remains of an old Vermont hill-town neighborhood. Eerie when the spring wind blows high in the treetops; mournful in a November snow.

5. First right on the downhill after notch, Jennings Rd.

6. Rowell Brook Rd. CAUTION: Hard right turn on downhill onto Wild Hill Rd.

7. Road becomes paved on downhill; condition poor, with cracks.

Redwing blackbird–lined Middle Brook is all that remains of a tongue of Lake Hitchcock, which once extended from Lake Fairlee to about a mile beyond West Fairlee Center. Today the car-free paved road following the languid brook makes for an easy four-mile pedal to look over Nathaniel Niles Pyramid in the West Fairlee burying ground. Beyond that point the incline up to the humble graves at Scruton Cemetery demands far more sweat equity and perhaps even a few dismounts. But surely Scruton is abandoned New England at its most evocative, and a world apart.

Note: In the fall, a commotion rising from the valley between Old Buffalo and Tebbetts Notch may break the silence of the woods through here. Ignore it; it's just one-ton Russian boars being hunted from armored personnel carriers at a private game preserve.

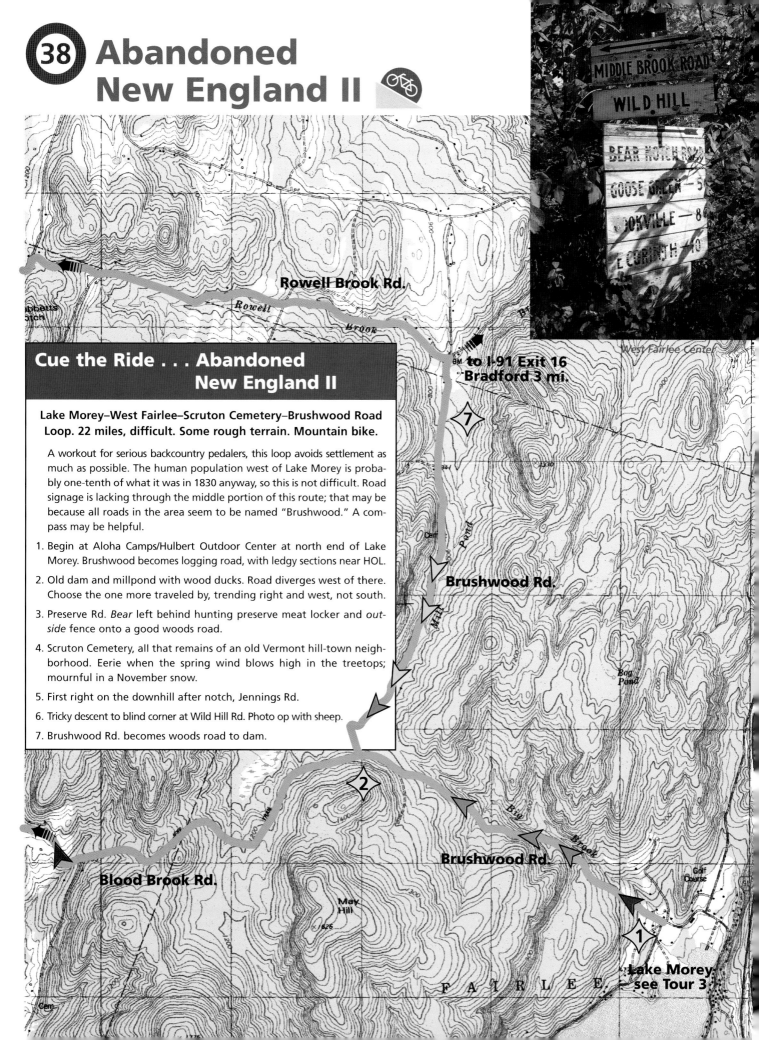

(38) Abandoned New England II

Cue the Ride . . . Abandoned New England II

Lake Morey–West Fairlee–Scruton Cemetery–Brushwood Road Loop. 22 miles, difficult. Some rough terrain. Mountain bike.

A workout for serious backcountry pedalers, this loop avoids settlement as much as possible. The human population west of Lake Morey is probably one-tenth of what it was in 1830 anyway, so this is not difficult. Road signage is lacking through the middle portion of this route; that may be because all roads in the area seem to be named "Brushwood." A compass may be helpful.

1. Begin at Aloha Camps/Hulbert Outdoor Center at north end of Lake Morey. Brushwood becomes logging road, with ledgy sections near HOL.

2. Old dam and millpond with wood ducks. Road diverges west of there. Choose the one more traveled by, trending right and west, not south.

3. Preserve Rd. *Bear* left behind hunting preserve meat locker and *outside* fence onto a good woods road.

4. Scruton Cemetery, all that remains of an old Vermont hill-town neighborhood. Eerie when the spring wind blows high in the treetops; mournful in a November snow.

5. First right on the downhill after notch, Jennings Rd.

6. Tricky descent to blind corner at Wild Hill Rd. Photo op with sheep.

7. Brushwood Rd. becomes woods road to dam.

Rowell Brook Rd.

Rowell Brook

to I-91 Exit 16
Bradford 3 mi.

West Fairlee Center

Brushwood Rd.

Bog Pond

Blood Brook Rd.

May Hill

Brushwood Rd.

Big Brook

Golf Course

Lake Morey –
see Tour 3

FAIRLEE

MIDDLE BROOK ROAD
WILD HILL
BEAR NOTCH ROAD
GOOSE GREEN – 5
OOKVILLE – 8
E CORINTH – 0

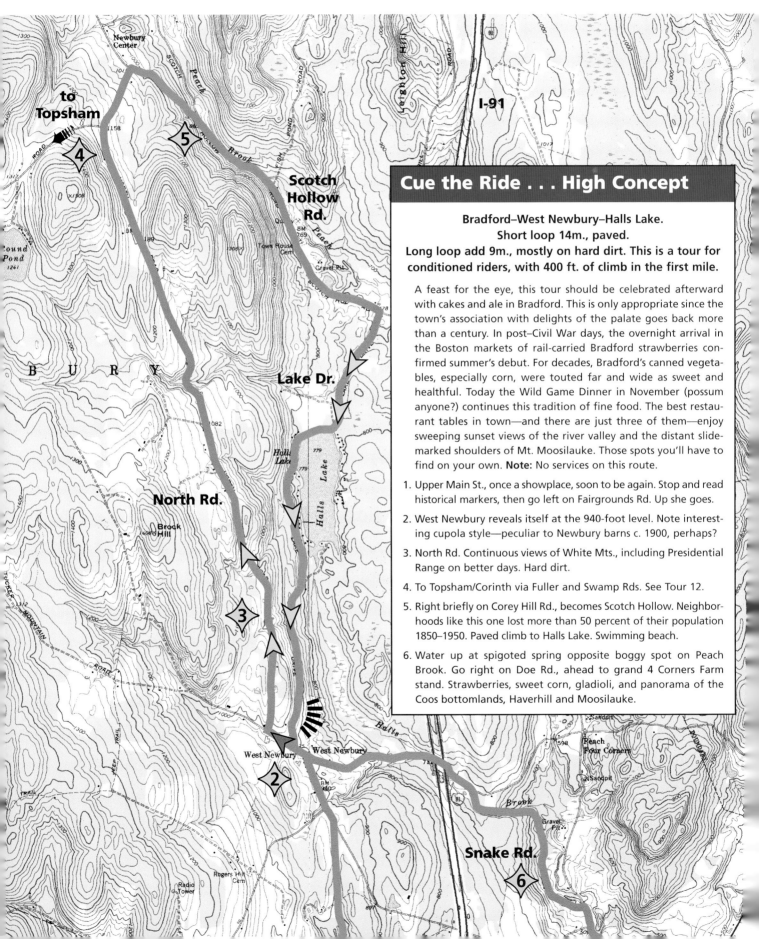

39 High Concept
Bradford-West Newbury

Cue the Ride . . . High Concept

**Bradford–West Newbury–Halls Lake.
Short loop 14m., paved.
Long loop add 9m., mostly on hard dirt. This is a tour for conditioned riders, with 400 ft. of climb in the first mile.**

A feast for the eye, this tour should be celebrated afterward with cakes and ale in Bradford. This is only appropriate since the town's association with delights of the palate goes back more than a century. In post–Civil War days, the overnight arrival in the Boston markets of rail-carried Bradford strawberries confirmed summer's debut. For decades, Bradford's canned vegetables, especially corn, were touted far and wide as sweet and healthful. Today the Wild Game Dinner in November (possum anyone?) continues this tradition of fine food. The best restaurant tables in town—and there are just three of them—enjoy sweeping sunset views of the river valley and the distant slide-marked shoulders of Mt. Moosilauke. Those spots you'll have to find on your own. **Note:** No services on this route.

1. Upper Main St., once a showplace, soon to be again. Stop and read historical markers, then go left on Fairgrounds Rd. Up she goes.

2. West Newbury reveals itself at the 940-foot level. Note interesting cupola style—peculiar to Newbury barns c. 1900, perhaps?

3. North Rd. Continuous views of White Mts., including Presidential Range on better days. Hard dirt.

4. To Topsham/Corinth via Fuller and Swamp Rds. See Tour 12.

5. Right briefly on Corey Hill Rd., becomes Scotch Hollow. Neighborhoods like this one lost more than 50 percent of their population 1850–1950. Paved climb to Halls Lake. Swimming beach.

6. Water up at spigoted spring opposite boggy spot on Peach Brook. Go right on Doe Rd., ahead to grand 4 Corners Farm stand. Strawberries, sweet corn, gladioli, and panorama of the Coos bottomlands, Haverhill and Moosilauke.

West Newbury,
Lafayette Range in the distance

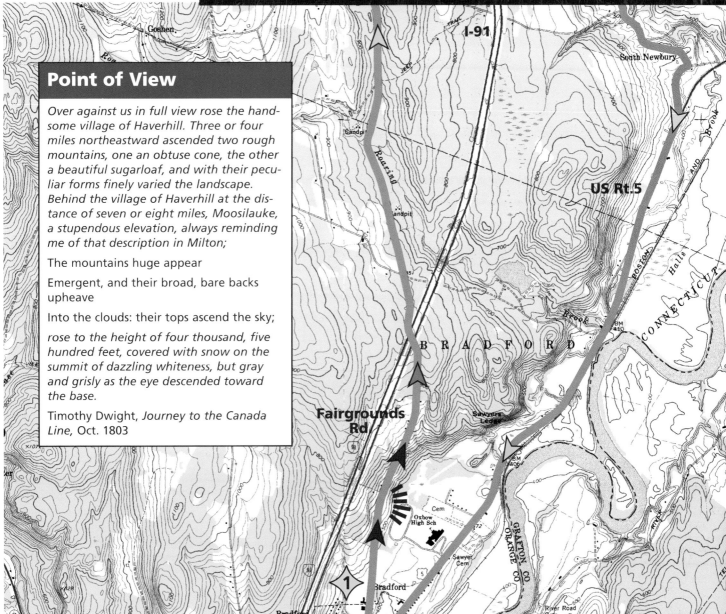

Point of View

*Over against us in full view rose the hand-
some village of Haverhill. Three or four
miles northeastward ascended two rough
mountains, one an obtuse cone, the other
a beautiful sugarloaf, and with their peculiar forms finely varied the landscape.
Behind the village of Haverhill at the distance of seven or eight miles, Moosilauke,
a stupendous elevation, always reminding
me of that description in Milton;*

The mountains huge appear

Emergent, and their broad, bare backs
upheave

Into the clouds: their tops ascend the sky;

*rose to the height of four thousand, five
hundred feet, covered with snow on the
summit of dazzling whiteness, but gray
and grisly as the eye descended toward
the base.*

Timothy Dwight, *Journey to the Canada
Line*, Oct. 1803

40 Stairway to Heaven, Strafford

Unlike the Parthenon and Chartres, the Strafford Town House was not built solely for worship. Instead, its promoters had to strike a compromise between sermonizing and secularizing in order to pay for it. New England small towns often did so because they couldn't afford more than one major public building. Even so, it took Strafford elders twenty years to convince a majority of voters to tax themselves to pay for a multi-use meeting place.

Construction began in the summer of 1799, when stone from nearby outcrops and handy glacial erratics was split for the foundation. Under the direction of master builder Levi George, oxen hauled logs to the knoll-top site for trimming out with broad axes. Lighter framing members were sawn by a water-powered up-and-down blade, probably at a mill at what later was to be known as Old City. Craftsman George had been called to Strafford after supervising similar big jobs in Salisbury and Canaan, N.H.

According to Gwenda Smith, whose 1992 book *The Town House* is the bible of this masterwork, the building's projecting square tower and front, rather than side, main door indicate the structure is transitional in the order of New England public architecture. Civil and sacred spheres diverged more clearly in America soon after 1800, and a number of existing buildings in the Town House style were converted to single-denomination houses of worship. This happened in 1830 at nearby Thetford Hill, when a townhouse was rolled across the street from the green to become today's Congregational Church. In Strafford, multi-use persisted much longer and therefore so did the structure's original conception, which has become iconic in the extreme. The only exterior modification was undertaken in 1935. Desperately in need of maintenance funds in the hollow of the Great Depression, the building's trustees accepted a cash gift and three clock faces that came with it.

In the summer of 1800, the Town House's steeple was topped off with a seven-foot swallow-tailed weathervane that still pivots today. After box-style pews had been auctioned off to townspeople, joiners began work on the interior. Pews near the pulpit had sold briskly at over $100 each, while spaces in the upper gallery brought about $30 apiece—big money two hundred years ago. As with the levy for the superstructure, buyers presumably were permitted to settle up in wheat, livestock, potash, or rarest of the rare, hard money.

Pew purchasers belonged to various denominations, each with the right to hold services throughout the day on Sunday on a rotating basis. Since they had bought thither and yon, during a service, the worshipful in smaller sects probably were stranded about the room like small islands. Above the pulpit, a sounding board—now removed—helped bridge the distance between pastor and flock.

By 1880 the town's A-list, the Universalists, had consolidated themselves at a church in South Strafford. It was just one more sign the Town House had slipped from favor with the pious. By this time, it more often housed social and political affairs. Secularity triumphed a few years later, and the pulpit and pews on the ground floor were removed. Fortunately, traditionalists managed to fight off a proposal to drop a ceiling, which would have halved the space horizontally. Nonetheless, with the addition of furniture made at a Pompanoosuc factory, the building became fully realized as a hall, complete with a proscenium. The Town House was now suitably fitted out for costume parties, cornet band concerts, and dramaturgy of every type. In the 1970s, the spindle-topped pews in the galleries were the beneficiary of thoughtful restoration, gracing the interior and giving it an enhanced early nineteenth-century mood.

Today, except for town meeting in March, the building is closed during winter. In warmer seasons, its first and second stories are

opened to a few select low-impact musical and social events and to the nuptials of one or more bona fide Strafford natives. Strangely then, while the exterior has thousands of lenses trained on it each year, few eyes get to glimpse the Town House's interior splendors. Despite its august elevation over the Strafford Common, viewing this masterpiece does not awe visitors the way castles and cathedrals do. The Town House's clapboarding and paned window treatment are too familiar, particularly to us New Englanders, to do that. Instead, these elements make it a relaxing building to be around, with just a hint of tension—

Robinson Cemetery, July

rather like seeing somebody we know up on stage getting an award. We look at it up there as we would a friend, but not a close friend, as the Town House doesn't exactly gather us to it. Like an old Vermont farmer, it is too spare to do so and from another age anyhow. Always in performance and always an award winner, after posing for the photographers, the Strafford Town House talks to us of time and its uses. It says, "Use time well, as I have done."

The Town House

Cue the Ride . . . Stairway to Heaven

Strafford–Kibling Hill–Strafford Loop.
14 miles, very demanding. Long, steep hills. Hybrid bike.

A real workout for a ride of only 14 miles, this ascent passes through various anterooms of paradise before closing with a 600-ft. climb to Kibling Hill. From there, a hilltop beckons.

1. Brook Rd., a walking hill. Paved to Rock Bottom Rd.

2. Vista best seen in early morning light. Robinson Farm in same family since 1700s.

3. Shaded climbs through the centuries.

4. Potash Rd., Tunbridge 2.3m. See Tour 35. Turkey flocks frequent these woods.

5. Ancient carriage track leads steeply uphill from small parking area. Follow it on foot.

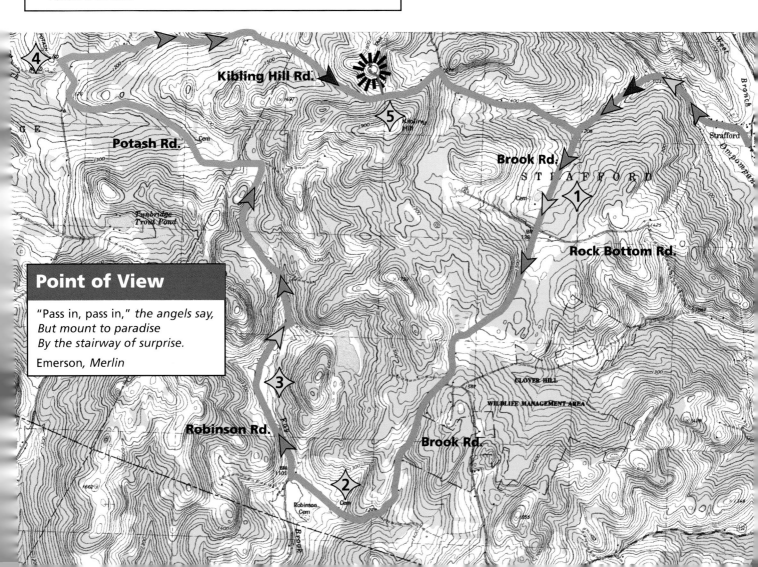

Point of View

"Pass in, pass in," *the angels say,*
But mount to paradise
By the stairway of surprise.
Emerson, *Merlin*

Afterword

Oh, the places you've *been*! But now where to? Off to Private Idaho's of your own finding, of course. And while you're doing that, I'll be out on reconnaissance missions of my own, uncovering more walks, hikes and lore for *Paradise Underfoot*.

I'll wrap up what I find in all the legends that wouldn't fit here: the Indian centuries, Eleazar "Slick Willy" Wheelock, New Connecticut, Dartmouth University (yes), the Vermont treasure hunting mania, America's first power walker Alden Partridge of Norwich, Woodstock in the Gilded Age, Justin Morrill's fuchsia house, and Benton MacKaye and his Appalachian Trail. Plus where to find everybody's favorite party animal—the MOOSE! (And all the geology you can stand of course.) Fun stuff all around.

What you might also do in the meantime is try to keep the Upper Valley a secret. I couldn't, and still can't.

Baker Library, Dartmouth College

Bibliography

Roadside Geology of Vermont and New Hampshire, B.B. Van Diver. Mountain Press Pub., 1987. Big Bang and after. Keep a copy in the glove compartment.

Written in Stone, Chet and Maureen Raymo. Globe Pequot, 1989. Best starter text on US geology, with emphasis on the Northeast.

Hands on the Land: A History of the Vermont Landscape, Jan Albers. MIT Press, 2000. Illustrated in color. Save Vermont!

This American River, W.D. Wetherell, Editor. UPNE, 2002. A way-overdue Connecticut River anthology.

The Town House, Gwenda Smith. Strafford Historical Society, 1992. Tops.

Orford New Hampshire, A Most Beautiful Village, Alice Doan Hodgson, 1972. Old, but good, like Orford. Illustrated in color. Available from Orford Historical Society.

Turnpikes of New England, F.J. Wood. Branch Line Press. Reprint of 1919 original.

On the Road North of Boston, New Hampshire Taverns and Turnpikes, 1700-1900, Donna-Belle and James Garvin. N.H. Historical Society. Fully illustrated. 2003 edition includes map.

Lost Railroads of New England, R.D. Karr. Branch Line Press, 1996. Definitive and invaluable.

The Up-Country Line : Boston, Concord & Montreal RR to the New Hampshire Lakes and White Mountains, Edgar T. Mead. Stephen Greene Press, 1975. Source for Tour 11, Oliverian Branch. Mead also produced classics on the Woodstock RR and the Concord & Claremont line.

Green Mountain Copper, Collamer Abbott. Privately printed 1973. Superb photos. Scarce.

Royalton Vermont, Hope Nash, Royalton Historical Society, others, 1975. Quite possibly the finest American small town history ever written.

American Cassandra, A Life of Dorothy Thompson, Peter Kurth. Little, Brown, 1990. Almost as good as Mark Schorer's celebrated bio of Sinclair Lewis.

Lafayette, Hero of Two Worlds, various authors. University Press of New England, 1989. The art and majesty of the man and his farewell tour.

The Upper Valley, An Illustrated Tour, Jerold Wikoff. Chelsea Green, 1985. Meat and potatoes history for non-cyclists.

Blood Brook, A Naturalist's Home Ground, Ted Levin. Chelsea Green, 1992. The Fairlee quadrangle under the microscope. Take it along on Connecticut River rides and on Tours 37 & 38.

The American Bicycle, Pridmore and Hurd. Motorbooks International, 1995. Luscious photographs meet thorough research and good writing. To die for.

The Bicycle Comes to Hanover, Clyde E. Dankert, 1980. A retired professor's labor of love monograph; source of Fletcher family cycling history. Copy in Howe Library, Hanover. Thanks, Clyde.

Vermont Place Names: Footprints of History, Esther M. Swift, Stephen Greene Press, 1977. Chock full of lore.

Rt. 12, Pomfret.
Headed for Silver Lake, Barnard.

Long Distance Rides (see inside back cover map)

1. WOODSTOCK • BETHEL • WEST HARTFORD LOOP, 42 MILES.

This popular loop begins with a personal favorite, the perfectly delightful down-sun, downwind ten-mile ascent to Silver Lake, Barnard from Woodstock. The return features a second climb of 600' over five miles between West Hartford and North Pomfret.

Route: North on VT Rt.12, Woodstock to Bethel, 16m. From Bethel village east on VT Rt.107 to VT Rt.14 intersection, 4m. Go south on VT Rt.14 to bridge at West Hartford, 10m. Cross steel bridge (with AT), immediately go right on Pomfret Rd. to Hewitts Corner, 5m. Then left and south on County Rd. to Pomfret and Woodstock, 7 m.

2. WOODSTOCK • READING • PLYMOUTH AND RETURN, 58/76 MILES.

Off to see the Jenne Farm in Reading, climb The Alps, and roll on down into the Coolidge Homestead in Plymouth, returning via the same route. An additional 18-miles can be added by making a loop of West Bridgewater and Bridgewater Cors. via VT Rt.100 and US Rt.4, (use road map). However, no matter what the map might suggest, do not return to Woodstock by the insanely dangerous section of US Rt.4 east of Bridgewater Corners. (The Jenne Farm? You'll know it when you see it, first right —"Jenne Rd."—off VT Rt.106 in Reading.) Note: Tyson Road becomes Kingdom Road in Plymouth.

Route: VT Rt.106 south from Woodstock to Felchville, 14m. Tyson Rd. west over The Alps to VT Rt.100, 10m. North on VT Rt.100 to Plymouth Union/100A to Coolidge site, 5m.

3. WHITE RIVER JCT. • SOUTH ROYALTON • BROOKFIELD AND RETURN, 78 MILES.

Enjoy the glories of the bypassed White River valley, covered bridges and all, made possible by traffic-attracting I-89, which parallels it. Less hilly than other routes, the only heavy lifting comes in the middle of the ride with the climb to the Floating Bridge at Brookfield, followed by several bumps on the way back south to Randolph Center. To shorten the ride by the length of a marathon, begin at Sharon, Exit 2. For details of the route see Tour 36.

Route: VT Rt.14 north from White River Jct. to East Brookfield. Distances: Sharon 13m., VT Rt.107 22m., East Brookfield 37m. At East Brookfield go left on VT Rt.65 to Floating Bridge, 2m. From Brookfield take Ridge Rd. south to VT Rt.66/Randolph Center, 6m., then VT Rt.65 east to VT Rt.14, 3m. Return via VT Rt.14. Note: Extra caution should be used on the steep descent from Randolph Ctr.

4. SOUTH ROYALTON • STRAFFORD • TUNBRIDGE LOOP, 27 MILES. FROM WHITE RIVER JCT., 53 MILES.

Hill, hills and more hills. Then bridges, bridges and more covered bridges along the First Branch of the White River.

Route: Begin on the Green in SoRo, choosing either River Rd. or VT Rt.14 to Sharon. At I-89 ascend VT Rt.132 to South Strafford, 6m. At South Strafford go left on Justin Morrill Hwy to Strafford, 2m. Bear right in Strafford on Tunbridge Rd., climb up and over to VT Rt.110 in Tunbridge, 8m. Follow VT Rt.110 south to SoRo, 6m. Note: Justin Morrill Hwy, Tunbridge Rd. and Strafford Rd. are one in the same, names vary between towns. See also Tour 40.

5. NORWICH • LAKE FAIRLEE • FAIRLEE AND RETURN, 45 MILES.

Popular with a group of breakfast riders who meet at the Hanover Inn, the meat of the journey is a 400' climb over three miles to Thetford Hill from Union Village.

Route: US Rt.5 Ledyard Bridge to VT Rt.132, 5m. VT Rt.132 west 2m., bear right into Union Village. Cross covered bridge on Academy Rd., climb to Thetford Hill, 3m. Left on VT Rt.113 to Post Mills, 7m. Right on VT Rt.244, east along Lake Fairlee and down to US Rt.5 at Ely, 6m. Left and north to Fairlee, 3m. Return via US Rt.5 or NH Rt.10.

6. BRADFORD • WAITS RIVER • TOPSHAM LOOP, 32 MILES. FROM LEDYARD BRIDGE, 77 MILES.

A lengthened version of Tour 13, this route includes several miles of hard dirt in Topsham. An all-paved loop can be made by staying on US Rt.302 (limited shoulder) to Groton and returning to Topsham/Corinth via Topsham/Powder Springs Rd. Note: The classic Waits River steeple and barns photo is taken from Pike Hill Rd. See Tour 13.

Route: Bradford, I-91 Exit 16 west on VT Rt.25 to US Rt.302. Distances: Waits River, 10m., Cross Road cutoff to US Rt.302, 15m. Go east on US Rt.302 .5m, then right on Willey Hill Rd. (dirt) to East Topsham, 4m. South on East Topsham Rd. to VT Rt.25, 5m. Return to Bradford, 6m.

7. WOODSVILLE • BARNET • GROTON LOOP, 35 MILES. FROM BRADFORD, 61 MILES.

The moderate climb from the valley at Monroe to West Barnet makes this a recommended route for road bikers on the lookout for the middle way. Maximization of views can be had by adding a loop of Harveys Lake via Roy Mountain Rd. (dirt), halfway between Barnet Center and West Barnet. Minimization comes in the way of the absence of auto traffic throughout. Note: No more dangerous corner exists in the region than the blind, steeply downhill intersection of Peacham Rd. and US Rt.302 in Groton. See also Tour 29.

Route: NH Rt.135 north from Woodsville to Monroe, 8m., cross to Vermont. North on US Rt.5 to Barnet, 3m., left on West Barnet Rd. to Harveys Lake, 5m. At south end of West Barnet village go right on Peacham-Barnet Rd. to South Peacham, 1m. Go left on Peacham Rd. to US Rt.302 in Groton, 8m. USE EXTREME CAUTION AT INTERSECTION. Left on US Rt.302 to Wells River, 10m.

8. PROUTY CENTURY, 100 MILES.

Each July for over twenty years Upper Valley walkers and riders have toured the Connecticut Valley countryside while raising money for the Norris Cotton Cancer Center in memory of Audrey Prouty. The Prouty Century is the route followed by the most dedicated of the cyclists.

Route: North from the Dartmouth Medical School in Hanover on NH Rt.10 to Orford, 15m. Right on NH Rt.25A over Mt. Cube to Wentworth, 16m. Left on NH Rt.25 to Warren, 6m., and Haverhill, 15m. NH Rt.10 north to Woodsville, 10m. Cross to Vermont, go left and south on US Rt.5 to East Thetford, 28m. Cross to N.H., go right on River Rd. to NH Rt.10. Hanover, 10m.

Note: For detail, use state road maps